The Scent of Jasmine

The Scent of Jasmine

Reflections for Peace
in Everyday Life

Patricia McCarthy, C.N.D.

*With love, in Him
David
(This is good — try it for
weekly readings)*

A Liturgical Press Book

THE LITURGICAL PRESS
Collegeville, Minnesota

1199

Cover design by Fred Petters

2	3	4	5	6	7	8	9

Library of Congress Cataloging-in-Publication Data

McCarthy, Patricia, 1944–
    The scent of jasmine : reflections for peace in everyday life / Patricia McCarthy.
       p.   cm.
    ISBN 0-8146-2332-8
    1. Church year—Prayer-books and devotions—English.
2. Peace—Religious aspects—Christianity.   3. Catholic
Church—Prayer-books and devotions—English.   I. Title.
BX2178.M37   1996
242'.3—dc20
                                     95-30480
                                         CIP

*It is right to keep
the secret of a king, yet
right to reveal and publish
the works of God.
(Tobit 12:7; The Jerusalem Bible)*

To Mary Margaret, Christina, Kathleen,
Katherine, Patricia, and
all our children.
May we leave them a legacy of peace.

CONTENTS

FOREWORD

The Song of the Dove

The voice of my beloved!
    Look, he comes,
leaping upon the mountains,
    bounding over the hills.
My beloved is like a gazelle
    or a young stag.
Look, there he stands
    behind our wall,
gazing in at the windows,
    looking through the lattice.
My beloved speaks and says to me:

"Arise, my love, my fair one,
    and come away;
for now the winter is past,
    the rain is over and gone.
The flowers appear on the earth;
    the time of singing has come,
and the voice of the turtledove
    is heard in our land.
The fig tree puts forth its figs,
    and the vines are in blossom;
    they give forth fragrance.
Arise, my love, my fair one,
    and come away.
O my dove, in the clefts of the rock,
    in the covert of the cliff,

> let me see your face,
>   and let me hear your voice;
> for your voice is sweet,
>   and your face is lovely."

(Song of Solomon 2:8-14)

The voice of God is always sweet, even when it is challenging. The Bridegroom is always lovely to the bride, even when he hangs disfigured on a cross.

The voice of the Spirit rings and whispers through the chapters of this book. In some chapters the Lover comes "leaping upon the mountains, bounding over the hills," overriding centuries of rationalizations and inertia, summoning the beloved to total union now. In other chapters the voice of the Bridegroom whispers with passionate gentleness, encouraging the bride to put off her fears, to waken quietly from sleep, to arise and step into the springtime, for the winter is past, the rains are over and gone, the flowers appear on the earth, and the time of singing has come.

This is a passionate book, passionate with the daily passion couples bring to life together in love. It is very much a "daily-life book," a book about living love daily as if each day were love's only chance. It gazes through the windows of liturgical feast days and civic holidays; it peers through the lattices of intertwining yearly events: school openings and graduations, June weddings and winter's hazards for the homeless. It is a book conscious of time: Advent, Lent, and Easter, and Ordinary Time made extraordinary by the incarnation of the Word of God. The Word made flesh in a woman's body, in Mary, the Mother of God, is flesh among us still. He "stands behind our wall" of human flesh. He speaks through the lives of saints and prophets, of martyrs and those whom the world calls misfits. He speaks through the pages of this book with passionate appeal.

The Lover speaks, and his words are always the same, "Arise, my beloved, my fair one, and come away." For the Church is beautiful, human beings are beautiful. Even in our mediocrity and our sinfulness we are beautiful. Even in our apathy we are able to rise. Even constrained by our fears and our selfishness, we give forth a fragrance that draws the Bridegroom to our side. And this fragrance can become the "scent of jasmine"—the pleasing odor of a life, a day, a moment offered as a sacrifice in love.

If this book did nothing else but teach us to peer through the lattices of family and cultural life, of business affairs and political challenges, from which "the very web of our existence is woven," and to find the Bridegroom there, it would be life-transforming. But it does more. It attunes us to listen to the voice of the Bridegroom speaking with the urgency of his immediate desire. It sounds the note of his demand in this pressing time of his presence, in this available place of our surrender. It is the voice of a passion that cannot wait, a passion calling us to accept the next step of his seduction and to surrender what he asks of us now.

In these times of violence and war, the Bridegroom calls us to peace. "Learn from me for I am gentle and humble of heart, and I will give you rest." In these days of dependence on power and deterrence, he invites us to be one with him in powerlessness, in the vulnerability of the lover.

This is the call to undivided self-bestowal, to freedom from all cultural conditioning and concerns, from all lesser loyalties and loves, to absolute adoration of God. It is a call to kneel to God alone and to refrain from kneeling to the false gods of materialism, militarism, and nationalism.

The voice of this book is the voice of the Lamb of God, offered for the sin of the world. It is the voice of the Bridegroom appealing to his bride to join him on the passionate bed of his cross, to offer with him the act of love that heals and gives life to the world. It is the voice of Jesus, rejected Messiah and friend of the poor, man of nonviolence and liberator from fear, passionate lover and prince of peace. In this book the voice of the dove is heard in our land, luring to love, promising peace.

Fr. David M. Knight

ACKNOWLEDGMENTS

Since this book covers experiences which span my entire lifetime, I cannot possibly thank everyone who has had a hand in it. I thank my parents and family for always welcoming and even encouraging the unexpected, for their love and support. My religious community, the Congregation of Notre Dame of Montreal, commissioned me to put all my energies into peace education—for this and for the freedom which has always accompanied my life in community, I am grateful. Special gratitude to those sisters with whom I share a praying, vibrant community life. Many of my friends and students will find themselves in this book—for their inspiration, thanks. *The Providence Visitor* was my first publisher; I thank Father Stan Nakowicz for the opportunity for my monthly column. Father David Knight of Memphis has been a good friend and excellent editor from the beginning—deepest thanks. Finally, I would like to express my gratitude to Father Michael Naughton, O.S.B., of The Liturgical Press for his willingness to read an unsolicited manuscript from an unknown author.

JANUARY TO MARCH: INTRODUCTION

Jesus, Incarnate Word, be here among us.

Jesus is the Incarnate Word of God. Jesus is God and Jesus is human. Jesus is with us, among us now and for all eternity if we choose to accept him. It is extraordinary that God became one of us. Faith and faith alone verifies this truth; there is no merely rational proof.

Our lives are spent in the living acceptance of this reality of God being among us. Every breath we draw, every thought we ponder, and every action we perform are the ways we believe or the ways we deny this reality. Life with God Incarnate is the basis of Christianity. It is also the basis of this book. The theme of this book is the person of Jesus and our relationship with him. No word of peace or cry against violence is uttered apart from the Word of God in Jesus Christ. No action for peace or resistance against injustice is taken apart from the presence of the man of peace, Jesus.

January

We begin this book with an act of faith in this incarnation of God, with an act of faith that Mary is the Mother of God. The Church begins the calendar year with a celebration of this mystery on January 1. *Jesus, Son of God and Son of Mary, be here among us.*

The Baptism of Jesus the following week heightens our awareness of the gift of our baptism. It reminds us of what our faith tells us about baptism and of the responsibilities that are ours because of this gift. *Jesus, life of Christians, be here among us.*

To be a Christian is to model our life on the life of Christ. We need to learn how to do this. Through the ages people of God of all nationalities and faiths have taught us the message of Jesus. His clearest message was that love has no limits. He taught us to love without counting the cost, to love even to the point of suffering violence without retaliating. Dr. Martin Luther King Jr. gave us an example of living the gospel call to love in a nonviolent manner as Jesus did. *Jesus, man of nonviolence, be here among us.*

Jesus taught us to love all people in all places and in all stages of growth, even our enemies, even those who harm or threaten us. As followers of Jesus, we try to be faithful to this call to universal love. We love life in the womb and life in the slum, life in prison and life in a nursing home. *Jesus, sanctifier of all life, be here among us.*

February

As January began with a celebration of life, February begins with a celebration of light—Christ's light. The Feast of the Presentation, or Candlemas Day, reminds us of our call to be the light of the world on the most ordinary of days. *Jesus, light in the darkness, be here among us.*

Because of the Incarnation, the light of Christ is diffused throughout the world, shining out in those people who remain faithful to Christ's way of loving, of enduring evil with love. On February 6 the Church holds up before our eyes Paul Miki and twenty-five companions who suffered persecution in Japan in the sixteenth century. *Jesus, strength of martyrs, be here among us.*

People of different faiths can also be light in the darkness, reflecting and living in the light of God. We learn from them. One of these faithful ones was Etty Hillesum, a Dutch Jewish woman who endured the persecution of the German army during the Second World War. As her world crumbled around her, Etty fell in love with a passionate God. She met the passion of God with the passion of a woman in love. Love is stronger than death, and death's darkness could not extinguish her light. *Jesus, passionate lover, be here among us.*

Our Incarnate God showed us the way to be light and life for others. His passion knew no bounds, his determination no limits. Jesus faced evil in the desert and spoke clearly against the powers that corrupt. He resisted their temptations and threw off their dominance for ever. There is only one way to justice—the way of God. Like Jesus, we risk the dangers of the desert to speak clearly our no to violence and power. *Jesus, prophet in the desert, be here among us.*

March

The desert decisions are what led Jesus to Calvary a few years later. He was crucified because he refused to cooperate with evil and its illusion of power. During Lent we concentrate on our suffering God. We stay close to him; we must learn from him how to die so that others may live. *Jesus, suffering servant, be here among us.*

Many Christians have learned this lesson of dying. Archbishop Romero of El Salvador was the good shepherd to his people, laying down his life for his sheep. *Jesus, friend of the poor, be here among us.*

The surrender to death will only come if the surrender has been lived all through life. Humanity's first act of absolute surrender took place in the heart of a young girl from Galilee two thousand years ago. When the Virgin Mary gave her yes to the angel Gabriel, she opened the door of surrender to all of us. If we wish to bear the Christ, we must surrender. *Jesus, desire of virgins, be here among us.*

Out of love Jesus lived with us, and out of love Jesus died for us. He came to do his Father's will, not his own. He came to love, not to be loved; to serve, not to be served. For this he was crucified. *Jesus, rejected Messiah, be here among us.*

January 1

THE SOLEMNITY OF MARY, MOTHER OF GOD

The calendar year in the West begins on January 1. The Church in the West celebrates the Feast of the Solemnity of Mary, Mother of God, on that day. In God's plan there are no coincidences. We begin our year with Mary.

It has been only seven days since Christmas, the feast of the incarnation of God in Jesus Christ. The Christmas trees are still up in our homes, candles in our windows pierce the dark winter nights, and manger scenes grace our mantles and churches. It has been seven days of sharing in the song of the angels as the *Gloria* was sung every day at Mass.

This day we look more closely at the Mother in the crèche. Mary, who was one of us, a human person, became the Mother of God. It was impossible and improbable.

A four-year-old child, pointing to a picture of Christ on her living room wall, asked: "Did you know that Jesus was God?"

"Yes, I knew that."

She continued, "Did you know that Mary was his mommy?"

"Yes, I knew that also."

"She was a mommy just like my mommy?"

"Yes."

"I don't get it. How could she have God? How could God make God?"

We are in the same position as the four-year-old child who just didn't "get it." This is mystery. Let us not be so used to the story that we become unmindful of the extraordinary way that God came among us: through a young woman from an oppressed people in a poor town.

The God of power and majesty, of omnipotence and wonder, the God who called prophets and formed covenants with our ancestors, the God of creation and revelation became one of us in the incarnation of Jesus Christ, who was born of a woman. How can we really "get it"? Nothing can prove this fact—it is mystery lived in faith, it is gift. The giver was God, but the one through whom God chose to give this gift was Mary. Through Mary we receive Christ.

As we begin this new year, let us pause in the presence of this mystery and acknowledge that Mary gave birth to the Son of God, to the praise and glory of God, for the redemption of all of us.

To admit that Jesus was the child of Mary and the Son of God implies that since we also are God's children, we are brothers and sisters of Christ and of one another. We are brought into intimate relationship with Mary because of the intimate relationship we have with Christ. And we are brought into the mystery of intimate relationship with one another. Let us pause in the presence of mystery.

In our time January 1 is also celebrated as the World Day of Prayer for Peace. If we embrace life based on the Incarnation, peace must be our way. Peace is our guide for redeeming the times. How can we not live in peace with one another and still claim to acknowledge our bond as brothers and sisters in Christ? War, racism, bigotry, prejudice, injustice, and hatred cannot coexist with the love and care of brother for sister and sister for brother.

We begin our year in truth and in the search for truth. The fundamental truth is that God is One, and this wonderful God of ours became one of us in Jesus Christ. Fidelity to this truth allows us to begin our year confidently, without fear. Christ's light dispels the darkness of fear and exposes its impotency. Fidelity to this truth compels us to begin our year in compassionate love and tolerance of one another. Mary, Mother of the Son of Peace, can lead us through the divisions within ourselves, the isolation and separation from one another. In God there are no divisions, and we are now and for all times in God.

Jesus, Son of God and Son of Mary, be here among us.

Reflection

1. Do I believe that Jesus Christ is God? What difference does this make in my life?

2. Do I believe that, because of the incarnation of Christ, all people are my brothers and sisters? What difference does this make in my life?

3. Do I believe that "in God there are no divisions"? Are there divisions in my life? What is one division to which I can bring the oneness of God?

The First Sunday after Epiphany

THE BAPTISM OF THE LORD

(When Epiphany is transferred to a Sunday that falls on January 8 or 9 the Baptism of the Lord is transferred to the Monday immediately following.)

Being a Christian requires work. It doesn't just come automatically after baptism any more than a successful marriage necessarily follows a wedding. By our baptism we commit ourselves to putting on the mind and heart of Christ. For those of us who were baptized as infants, it is only as adults that we can deliberately live out this commitment.

Attending Mass on Sunday, sending our children to Catholic schools, and contributing to the Church are not the extent of the responsibilities of baptized Christians. In fact, we can do all of those things and still be living lives apart from the way of Christ.

We are baptized into Christ. To give flesh and blood to this union means that we try to act as Christ would in every circumstance of our personal, family, business, and social life. To give flesh and blood to this union means that we put time and effort into trying to understand the way of Christ and to live the way of Christ.

As baptized Christians we determine our course of action in any given situation by Christ's criteria. Before we act, we consider how Christ might act in the same circumstances. The standards of society or the opinions of other persons are not the measure of our decisions. Our faith requires us to think and act as Christ would. We strive to be free from social pressures and mores as our motivations for action.

This is a wonderful and challenging call of our faith, a call that we often abandon. Too many times we allow others to influence the course of our actions and just go along with their decisions. To renew our commitment to baptism is to renew our willingness to think for ourselves.

Our baptism calls us to question everything, to hold up everything we do to the light of Christ's teachings as revealed in Scripture and in the doctrines of our Church. As Catholics we believe in the teaching authority of the Church, but it is important here to distinguish between the official teachings of the Church and the practices of the Church. For example, slavery was never accepted as official doctrine of the Church, but many Catholics, including bishops, priests, and religious orders, had slaves. There was also widespread segregation within the Church, another practice that was clearly contrary to the teachings of Jesus. Many German Christians went along with anti-Semitism under Hitler. Many American Christians approved of the fire-bombing of Dresden, a city of refugees. Many Japanese Christians actively participated in the militarism of their government before Pearl Harbor.

How could this happen if people were trying to live every action according to the way of Christ? It could happen because too often Christians do not think independently and form their own opinions and consciences. They submit to the judgments of others, of their elected or appointed officials, of those in charge. They trust others to decide for them. They go along with the practices of society instead of putting into practice the teachings of Jesus.

Our baptism tells us that we can never do this. We can never surrender responsibility for our actions to anyone. We cannot surrender our consciences to any government official, to any priest, nun, teacher, doctor, father, mother, brother or sister. No one can act for us. We are other Christs. He alone is our standard.

Perhaps we have lived so long with Christianity that we think we know it completely. We need to take the time to realize we do not fully comprehend Christianity or understand perfectly all that being a Christian involves. We are disciples, always learning from the Master Teacher.

On a practical basis, what does this mean? It means that we daily read the Word of God and pray over it to understand the message of Christ. Some of us would never think of not hearing the news or the weather report every day or of not reading the newspaper; yet the most important task of our lives is to allow ourselves to be formed into the people of God, and we leave that to one hour on Sunday.

Being a Christian means that we take Christ seriously. We speak to him in the course of our daily lives and expect him to speak to us. As we go through each day making the hundreds of decisions that are part of it, we ask Christ to form us, to help us act on his word in making these decisions.

Jesus Christ allowed himself, the Son of God, to be baptized to show us the need for decisions and the responsibility and power of commitment. Our own baptism is a share in the very life and commitment of Christ. It calls for gratitude as well as courage.

Jesus, Life of Christians, be here among us.

Reflection

1. Being a Christian requires work. Can I make a list of my Christian "work" on an average day?

2. If the ways of Christ are not the ways of society, how do I learn the ways of Christ?

3. A disciple learns from the teacher. Who is Jesus to me? What do I do to learn from Jesus? What actions do I take to foster my ability to think like Jesus?

January 15

MARTIN LUTHER KING, JR.

In the United States this day commemorates the civil rights leader Dr. Martin Luther King, Jr. In our time and in our country, Dr. King consistently preached the gospel of Jesus, the gospel word of nonviolence.

No words of Jesus have been more ignored by Christians than the ones emphasized by Dr. King—love of enemies. He held before us the person of Jesus and insisted upon the practicality and truthfulness of the message of Jesus. Dr. King tried to help us see God in a new way: he tried to help us see the God of Jesus, the God who has made us all brothers and sisters in Jesus.

Ironically, Martin Luther King turned to a non-Christian for guidance in understanding the Christian message of love of enemies. A serious student of Mohandas Gandhi, Dr. King applied Gandhi's principles of nonviolence to the freedom struggle of blacks in the United States. He did this within the context of his call as pastor. He used to say that he received his goals from Christ and his tactics from Mahatma Gandhi.

To the anger of many of his black brothers and sisters, Martin Luther King's civil rights revolution centered on love of the enemy, and he preached the harsh reality of that love. He set about to free the blacks from oppression and the whites from being oppressors. He taught his people to forgive, to believe that there was more to their enemies than the evil they

inflicted, and to strive for their friendship, not their humilia-
tion. "To our most bitter opponents we say: We will match
your capacity to inflict suffering by our capacity to endure
suffering. We shall meet your physical force with soul force.
Do to us what you will, and we shall continue to love you."[1]

One of the greatest gifts of Dr. King's legacy was his actual strategy for organizing a nonviolent campaign. Each activity was undertaken only after careful and extensive study,
preparation, and prayer. The plan for each activity in the civil
rights struggle had four basic steps:

1. collection of facts of the injustices;
2. negotiation with the enemy;
3. self-purification by prayer and fasting;
4. direct action.[2]

In Dr. King's life we find numerous examples of the use of
this plan. In response to a violation of human rights, specific
charges first had to be determined. In Birmingham, Alabama,
the refusal to serve blacks at lunch counters in department
stores was the problem. A decision had to be made whether
or not the injustice warranted intervention at this time. In
Birmingham the organizers for the blacks waited until after
a city election before beginning specific actions of protest. They
wanted to give the new administration a chance to correct the
situation.

Dr. King then began a series of meetings with the store-
owners to try to receive justice from them. Originally the
owners agreed to serve blacks as well as whites, but after a
few weeks they reversed their decision. Negotiations broke down
after five months and the work of protest seemed imminent.

Now the work moved from the city stores and mayor's
office to the churches. The people gathered to pray and prepare for the sacrifices involved in active resistance to injustice.
The plan of action for the citywide boycott of stores with
segregated lunch counters was devised, taught, and followed.
Daily prayer meetings and nonviolence training sessions be-

gan. The work of justice was a work of love in means as well
as goals.

The same process that is effective on a large scale works
on an individual basis. If we suffer offense from another person, we must look at the situation objectively and examine
the facts to see if there was an actual offense intended or if
it was just a misunderstanding. If there is a situation of injustice and it is serious enough to warrant our efforts, then
we move to the negotiating phase. We speak to those involved,
to those who are perpetrating the injustice. We try to help
the truth emerge; we try to negotiate an understanding.

If we meet with resistance to this attempt at reconciliation and justice, we deepen our prayers and fast or do penance for the resolution of the problem. Sometimes at this stage
impenetrable defenses can be dissolved and an impossible
problem can be solved.

However, if justice does not emerge after the fact-finding,
negotiating, and praying, then the active resistance begins
in a way consistent with the ethic of nonviolence. All actions
must be planned, and they must be peaceful in all ways. Revenge and violence have no place in active resistance. The
goal is truth for all, not victory for one.

It is crucial, if we would learn from history, that step four
(direct action) not be initiated apart from steps one, two, and
three (collection of facts, negotiation, and prayer). Both Gandhi
and King painfully acknowledged failures in their work due
to inadequate preparation of some of the people. Using the
nonviolence as nothing but a technique to achieve an immediate goal, many engaged in direct action without embracing
the philosophy of love of enemies and expressing the willingness to suffer for them.

Nonviolence is not merely a strategy for change; it is a
way of life based on the life of Jesus. It can be lived in the
personal, social, and political arenas of life, but it must be
lived consistently. To think that nonviolence can be lived in
some circumstances and not in others is to misunderstand nonviolence. Nonviolence is love in action; it is a reflection of

the all-inclusive love of God. No one is excluded from the love of God, and no one can be excluded from our love. Nonviolence is the lived expression of this belief.

Martin Luther King tried to live his life in fidelity to this belief and in fidelity to the command of Jesus to love one another as he loved us. Dr. King tried to put these words of Jesus into daily acts of justice and works of mercy. We do not honor Dr. King only by taking a holiday from school or work; we honor Dr. King by trying to understand his teachings and by reflecting upon his life so that we may learn to imitate and practice the principles for which he stood and the values for which he died.

Jesus, man of nonviolence, be here among us.

Reflection

1. Dr. King emphasized Jesus' command to love our enemies. Who are my enemies? Do I feed feelings of hatred or anger toward them? Do I make deliberate acts of love toward them?

2. Do I have friends who are of another race? Have I been in their homes and invited them to mine? Are my children being brought up in an environment in which they have the opportunity to play with and know children of other races and nationalities?

3. As I reflect on one serious conflict in my life, have I looked at the situation objectively, not just from my side? Have I talked to my opponent in this conflict? Have I tried to reach out in truth and in love for the good of all, not only for personal victory?

January 22

PRO-LIFE

Personal moral choices demand integrity and inner truthfulness. They are made in the direct light of what is good and just, not in the indirect light of what is merely expedient.

Only God is the direct light of truth, and all of us must expend considerable effort in our search for this truth and for God. Neither can be given to us by someone else. We can be inspired by the faith and wisdom of others. But we cannot see the light of God through the eyes of others only. A personal God demands a personal response. In daily life we live through this personal response in every moral decision and choice we make.

One specific area of moral decision-making that we should spend more time examining is our stand on pro-life issues. No word has been more misused in these times than "pro-life." In the name of supporting life, violent actions have been condoned, harsh judgments on others passed, and self-righteousness accepted.

Emotional reactions from both sides of the right-to-life debate detract from the issue. Fidelity to the search for truth brings us to focus on the issue, which is life: each person's God-given right to a life lived in dignity and respect, from beginning to end. As Christians we are called to value, nourish, and protect life at every stage and under all circumstances. The call to witness to a pro-life stand is all-encompassing. Pro-life means far more than being pro-birth or anti-abortion. Support for life in the womb is essential, but it is only the beginning of a daily, lifelong commitment to expressing by our actions the truth that each human life is precious to God.

Such a commitment requires us to protect the unborn child, to assist the unwed mother or the poor couple who are awaiting a birth in the grip of poverty, to look out for our neighbors with large families who may need assistance. It requires us to care for the increasing number of families that are unable to afford medical care. If we want to support life, we can no longer be comfortable with housing standards that decrease as income decreases. The elderly can no longer be someone else's problem. The homeless become our brothers and sisters, not merely undefined, unnamed "street people." Respecting life implies rejecting the death penalty, as we have been taught by our American bishops. How can we see the gift of God in an unborn child and not see the same gift, however marred by criminal actions, in this child who has grown into adulthood?

Finally, if we want to be consistent with the truth that each person is of inestimable value in the eyes of God and only God has the right to say when that life is to be completed, we must face the question of mass killing—the reality we call war. To support war is to abandon respect for the life of our enemies. If we are to be consistent in our respect for life, we cannot condone war. To think this way is to think as Christ does and not as others teach us to think. To think this way is challenging. To some it may seem new and different. But we must pursue truth even when it takes us beyond what we can easily understand.

Today we grab for the quick fix. To settle difficult international affairs, we use military force. To stop the growing crime rate, we cry for the death penalty. For troubled marriages, we seek divorce. For loneliness, we have an affair. And to settle the problem of an unexpected or unwanted pregnancy, we abort the "problem" without ever giving it the name of "child." As Christians we cannot sacrifice anyone in God's creation just to make life more convenient for ourselves. This is not Christianity.

Christianity is not about the quick fix—it is about peace with ourselves, with one another, and with God. Christianity proclaims this peace through love of friend and enemy alike. Christianity involves hard choices and decisions that cost, choices and decisions that have to be made all along the way if we are to make them at the crisis points of life.

Before we claim to be pro-life, let us study to see if we defend life whenever and however it is violated. If we really want to live the pro-life message, we have to look at our daily life to see if we are living in such a way that we support life in all its demands and varieties. The unborn child needs our support, but so does the unemployed husband, the battered wife, the mentally ill man, the frail elderly woman, and the young woman who has had an abortion. Jesus has told us how to respect life: "Just as I have loved you, you also should love one another" (John 13:34).

Jesus, sanctifier of all life, be here among us.

Reflection

1. As I consider the last three choices I have made in my life: (a) Did I act out of expediency? (b) Did I act out of a sense of justice and goodness?

2. What is my position on abortion? on the death penalty? on personal and domestic violence? on war? Are my positions consistent with the truth that each person is of inestimable value in the eyes of God?

3. Aside from my beliefs, what specific steps do I take to support life in all its stages?

February 2

THE PRESENTATION OF THE LORD

In our day of electricity, total darkness is rare. Every once in a while, due to a winter storm or a hurricane, or perhaps when camping on a starless night, we experience night in all its darkness. Then we appreciate the light of a single flashlight or of one candle. No matter how small the light, it dispels the darkness. It warms our spirits even if the flame is low.

Today we celebrate the light of Christ, the light of the nations proclaimed by Simeon when Mary and Joseph bring Jesus to the Temple to present him to God. Bearing a pair of turtledoves, the offering of the poor, the new parents come with their God and their son. Waiting in the Temple are Simeon and Anna, faithful people of the Old Covenant, both so in love with God that they recognize the Word of God when he comes into their midst, even though he is still only a child.

Simeon bursts into gratitude and praise of God, proclaiming: "My eyes have seen your salvation, which you have prepared in the presence of all peoples, a light for revelation to the Gentiles and for glory to your people Israel. This child is destined for the falling and the rising of many in Israel, and to be a sign that will be opposed so that the inner thoughts of many will be revealed—and a sword will pierce your own soul too" (Luke 2:30-32, 34-35).

Anna, bent from the years, lifts her voice with Simeon's. Day and night for many years her prayers and entreaties have

17

gone to God. She also sees the Messiah in the baby and speaks of him to anyone looking for the promised redemption. The time of salvation has come, and Anna is living the time fully.

Mary and Joseph simply stand in offering, open to all the possibilities that God will present through their son. Quietly they return to Nazareth so that Jesus can grow in their care until he is ready to allow his light to burn for others, even to extinction.

The story is simple—poor people being faithful to a custom of their religion. And yet, how much more than fidelity to custom does their story reveal! Mary, Joseph, Simeon, and Anna were doing on that day what they had done many times before: they were living their faith and expressing it through a ritual of offering and prayer. God chose that moment as a time of revelation. The ordinary became extraordinary. The activity of humans became the work of God. That is what we are celebrating on this feast.

The Presentation calls us to fidelity to the ordinary in expectation of its transformation into the holy. With the incarnation of Jesus Christ, God entered into humanity in such an extraordinary way that all life was forever changed. In the presentation in the Temple we begin to see the ramifications of this change. Not only is God among us, but all our actions can become part of the holy and the sacred. Our acts of kindness, tolerance, and justice bring light to this world struggling with the darkness of sin.

The Presentation calls us to be the light of Christ to one another so that the transformation of the ordinary may be revealed. Because of Christ, our eyes will see what they have never seen before, and our mouths will proclaim the presence of God in our midst. We ourselves become candles waiting for the light of Christ, prepared to be set on fire in love.

Jesus, light in the darkness, be here among us.

Reflection

1. What is one area of darkness in my personal, daily life? Am I willing to allow the light of Christ to penetrate this darkness? In a darkened room, light one candle and reflect in silence for fifteen minutes on this issue.

2. Is there one custom or practice of my religion to which I am especially faithful? What is the attraction of this practice? Can I celebrate my fidelity and God's fidelity over the years expressed through this practice?

3. What ordinary thing this day did God make extraordinary?

February 6

SS. PAUL MIKI AND COMPANIONS

In 1597, under dictator Hideyoshi, twenty-six Christians of Japan were martyred in Nagasaki. After being forced to march from Kyoto, a thirty-day journey, they were hung on crosses on a hill overlooking the port of Nagasaki and were killed by thrusts of bamboo spears.

It had been less than fifty years since St. Francis Xavier had arrived in Japan. Christianity had spread quickly, especially in the southern part of the country near Nagasaki. Seminaries, schools, and churches had been built and were flourishing. The early Jesuit missionaries were wise. They learned the culture and language of the Japanese and tried to teach the gospel apart from their own Spanish or Portuguese culture.

In the beginning the Christians were accepted by the government and allowed to practice their faith openly. However, in a sudden shift of mood, Hideyoshi banned Christianity and threatened death for any who practiced it. He arrested twenty-six men—brothers, priests, and laymen—intending to use them as an example to discourage Christianity in Japan. Beginning in Kyoto, the site of the arrests, the men began their month-long journey to Nagasaki, walking under the guard and jeers of the emperor's soldiers.

One of those arrested was Paul Miki, a thirty-three-year-old Jesuit and a zealous preacher. Rather than let himself be silenced by the arrest and the march from Kyoto, he used it as an opportunity to preach. All along the way he spoke and prayed with the people. His burning zeal to preach was being realized.

When the prisoners arrived at Nagasaki, Hideyoshi had chosen the highest hill in Nagasaki for their execution so as to make a public spectacle of their death. Twenty-six crosses were erected, and the men were tied to them. Hideyoshi intended to create fear in the people, many of whom he knew were Christians.

God had other plans. From their crosses the men sang psalms and hymns and prayed the *Our Father* and the *Hail Mary* in loud voices, inspiring faith in the Christians witnessing their tortures. Over four thousand took up the songs and prayers. The people of God were strong and joyful; there was no fear or intimidation in them.

It is customary in Japan for a brave warrior, a samurai, to speak before his death. Paul Miki asked permission to speak; here was his chance to preach from the pulpit of the cross. In a strong voice he began, "I am a Japanese and a brother of the Society of Jesus. I have committed no crime. The only reason I am condemned to die is that I have taught the gospel of our Lord Jesus Christ."[3] Paul encouraged any present who were not Christian, including his executioners, to embrace the faith. Then, in words similar to those of another thirty-three-year-old who was crucified with forgiveness of his enemies on his lips, Paul Miki said, "My religion teaches me to pardon my enemies and all who have offended me. I do gladly pardon the emperor and all who sought my death."[4]

In any age such witness of forgiving love is extraordinary. For the Japanese it was crucial to their understanding of the message of Christ. Paul Miki claimed his Japanese culture fully but went beyond the need to save face and revenge wrong. He preached love of enemies as his *jisei no uta* (farewell song of the samurai). Paul Miki is a saint not only for the Japanese but for the universal Church. We need to learn his story and tell it to our children. Our faith is incomplete until we understand as fully as he did Christ's lesson of forgiveness.

The words of preachers more famous than Paul Miki have long been forgotten. There is a reason why God let us know the story of this man and his final words and act of love. We remember not just to honor but to imitate.

The brutal execution of twenty-six courageous and faithful men became a scene of the triumph of love over evil. It nourished the seed of faith and kept it alive in Japan during two hundred years of persecution. There is no explaining the healing power of forgiving love. Only in the living does it become credible. Only in the living does it become the transforming yeast of hope for all society.

Jesus, strength of martyrs, be here among us.

Reflection

1. Do I ever reflect on the men and women who have died for their faith and thus fed my own life of faith? Who are the people today who are giving their lives for the faith?

2. Is there anyone I need to forgive? How will I begin the process of forgiveness?

3. Is there anyone of whom I need to ask forgiveness? How will I do this?

February 14

VALENTINE'S DAY

St. Valentine's Day seems to have been taken over by the greeting card companies, the candymakers, and the florists. Even when we live with people who know we love them, there is something special about a card or a gift of flowers to express the specialness of a relationship.

In Holland during World War II, there lived a woman who understood the need to speak words of love and to bring flowers to the one loved. A Dutch Jew, she was killed at Auschwitz in 1943 at the age of twenty-nine. Her name was Etty Hillesum.

As Etty's world was crashing around her, she grew from a fearful, unsure youth into a courageous and confident woman. While the circumstances of her life became more and more oppressive, her spirit became more and more liberated. What happened to change her? Etty fell in love with God, and that love carried her deeply into the pain of her people and freely into the arms of her God.

Etty was neither escaping from reality nor denying it. Religion was not a fantasy for her but a source of passion. She stood up to the suffering in her life and in the lives of all her friends and family, believing that God still loved and people were still lovable. She wrote in her journal: "To think that one small human heart can experience so much, oh God, so much suffering and so much love, I am so grateful to You,

God, for having chosen my heart, in these times, to experience all the things it has experienced.''

Etty's God was more real to her than her closest friends were. She knelt before God, spoke to God, wrote to God, and listened to God. Again in her journal: ''Alone for once in the middle of the night. God and I have been left together, and I feel all the richer and at peace for it.'' Etty lived with God.

Outside of Etty's apartment grew jasmine flowers, which she loved and lingered over in the mornings. Delicate and dazzling, they made her catch her breath with surprise. The jasmine became for her a symbol of beauty that no amount of evil could eradicate. ''I am with the hungry and the ill-treated and the dying every day, but I am also with the jasmine and with that piece of sky beyond my window; there is room for everything in a single life. For belief in God and for a miserable end.''

As life became more desperate in Holland and as the threat of extermination in the death camps came closer, Etty's passion increased. She longed to show her love for God; she trusted God, and she knew that God trusted her. After a storm had destroyed her jasmine flowers, she continued to believe that they still blossomed within her. She still carried the delicate flowers for her God.

> You [God] can see, I look after you, I bring you not only my tears and my forebodings on this stormy, gray Sunday morning, I even bring you scented jasmine. And I shall bring you all the flowers I shall meet on my way, and truly there are many of those. I shall try to make you at home always. Even if I should be locked up in a narrow cell and a cloud should drift past my small barred window, then I shall bring you that cloud, oh God, while there is still the strength in me to do so.[5]

The scent of jasmine was for Etty the symbol of trusting abandonment to God. To be the scent of jasmine is to be present in love to God for the sake of all the people of God. This Valentine's Day let us speak words of love to those we love and bring them flowers. Let us speak words of love to God and carry to God in our bodies the delicate scent of jasmine.

Jesus, passionate lover, be here among us.

Reflection

1. Have I ever fallen in love with God? When was I first aware of this? What are some of the highlights of this relationship?

2. How do I give expression to the passion I feel and choose for God? What is my jasmine?

3. How do I experience God's expression of passion for me? What are the flowers God sends me?

Ash Wednesday

DESERT PROTEST

"Let us fix our attention on the blood of Christ and recognize how precious it is to God his Father, since it was shed for our salvation and brought the grace of repentance to all the world" (Office of Readings for Ash Wednesday).

The Nevada Test Site, located sixty-five miles northwest of Las Vegas in Nye County, Nevada, is operated by the United States Department of Energy to provide an on-continent site for testing nuclear weapons. Until the temporary moratorium on nuclear testing declared in October 1993, tests were conducted approximately once every three weeks at a cost of six to seventy million dollars per test. The first atmospheric test was conducted in this 1,350 square-mile area on January 27, 1951.

The Nevada Desert Experience is a faith-based organization of Franciscan origin. It works to end nuclear weapons testing through a campaign of prayer, dialogue, and nonviolent direct action at the Nevada Test Site. People gather at the site many weekends of the year to reflect and pray. The group of people who have been planning the activities at the test site over the years give serious time to this element of the protest. For a one-hour protest march at the site, there are often two or three days of prayer and dialogue. Time is given to teaching or reinforcing awareness of the scriptural values inherent in the way of nonviolence. Time is also given to preparing for the actual protest action planned at the test site.

Before the action moves to the desert, the protesters ask permission from the Shoshone chief to go on tribal lands. Shoshone land was confiscated by the United States government for the test site. The Shoshone chief meets the protesters at the test site and gives them permits to pass onto Shoshone land.

Once the protesters are at the site, the prayer continues. This prayer is far more than a few words spoken by the group; it is a time for those present to walk amid the desert beauty in silent presence to their God. Following this prayer comes the walk across the cattle guard that is the line of trespass onto government property. This line is several miles from the first building at the test site. The local police are always notified of any intended act of civil disobedience before it happens. Over the course of the years the police and the protesters have become good friends as they have met in the desert.

The participants in the act of trespassing, which is the act of civil disobedience, are trained to respect the police and any others who may object to their action. All quick or threatening motions are avoided, violent comments and abusive language are prohibited, and courtesy and respect are shown to everyone. At the first sign of violence all activity ceases. These protests are the work of God, and they must be consistent with the ways of God. The act of protest must be understood and accepted as a call from God if it is to be undertaken in faith.

On the surface, a call to the desert could appear as an invitation to embrace comforting solitude amid the raw beauty of untrod sand and pebble. In every desert creature, color and texture carefully blend, designed for survival. But this is a new day; it is a new desert, a desert being destroyed by radiation and shock, a desert being bound and sold, prevented from producing and appropriated for greed.

Jesus went into the desert. He was the first to cross the line, to dare to look into the faceless reality of evil and say, "Worship the Lord your God, and serve only him" (Luke 4:8). Jesus went ahead of us to show us how to worship, how to be the people of God we were created to be. He knew we could never be human with one another as long as we had gods of metal and iron. He also knew that we could not disarm, that we could not emancipate our hearts from these false gods without living the truth of God.

The desert is the place within us where we affirm the truth of God and admit that it doesn't fit with the reality of destruction and violence. Going into this place doesn't demand heroism; it demands surrender to the awesome person of God and abandonment to the heart of God. From there the will and desires of God consume us, transforming hearts of stone into hearts of flesh and blood.

The desert is the place where we allow our hands to be bound and our bodies to be led into a holding cell. We go through the motions of being booked and charged with trespassing on federal property, knowing that the obvious is not the real. The ones in handcuffs are not the ones who are bound. Neither handcuffs nor jail nor death can capture the freedom of the surrendered heart.

Jesus has taught us that the meek will inherit the earth and that his way is the way of the powerless. A human person or even a large group of human persons challenging the power of a nuclear bomb looks ridiculous. To challenge the nuclear industry is to take on an impossible task. In Christ all things are possible.

Someone holds a crucifix high at the line of trespass, drawing the eyes of the marchers as they approach. Each one acknowledges the crucified Lord—some genuflect, some prostrate, some renew vows. Arms are outstretched, tears flow, songs are sung. He is the reason we are here.

We protest and witness and pray in the desert because we must stand for the ways of God, which are not the ways of destruction and death. We stand for no other reason than to bear witness to the uncompromising ethic of love for friend and enemy alike, which is the teaching of the Word of God.

Finally, when the arrests are made and the prayers finished, we leave the desert. We return to our daily routines to continue loving and serving one another. Having said no to the ways of evil, Jesus returned from the desert to minister to his people. Because of him, we do the same.

Jesus, prophet in the desert, be here among us.

Reflection

1. What do I know about civil disobedience? Do I prejudge as fanatics all who protest? Am I willing to take the time to learn the principles of nonviolent direct action?

2. Do I act helpless in the face of overwhelming societal patterns of consumerism, greed, and corruption? Do I act as if love is stronger than hate, the ways of Christ more powerful than the ways of society? Are my choices consistent with my beliefs?

3. Am I willing to go into the desert with Christ? to allow my preconceived ideas to be shattered? to risk being vulnerable to Christ? to surrender to transformation?

LENT: A TIME WITH JESUS

Mardi Gras is usually celebrated with a sense of "Eat, drink, and be merry, for tomorrow you fast." In the past, when the Church had standard regulations for fasting for all adults, there was a common sense of everyone sharing in the same penance once the season of Lent began on Ash Wednesday. If such practices created a sense of common prayer, they were good; if they created a sense of pressure and rigidity, they were not good.

The youngest children seemed to know it was a time to "give up." They stashed away their candy while their parents stashed away their alcohol. Flowers no longer graced the altars in church, the alleluias were silenced, and the general feeling was that of a collective holding of breath until the six weeks had finally passed. On Easter we could let out our breath—we had made it through another Lent.

Lent needs to be started with a "who," not a "what." Before we make our resolutions about what we are going to do without, we need to spend some time with the One with whom we are uniting during this season.

Jesus Christ came to this earth as a man. He grew up in a loving family. He studied the word of God, prayed and responded to God throughout his life. When he was about thirty years old, he began his relatively short time of ministry. He gathered twelve special friends and many other followers. He spent three years bringing his message of healing love to the people of Galilee, always giving priority to the poor and to those who needed healing of body and spirit.

Jesus did not come as just another preacher in a long line of prophets. Jesus came as the Messiah; he came for redemption. The way of redemption would be the way of God, the way of love. Jesus came to bring the Good News and to be the Good News.

Jesus Christ was not accepted, and the price he paid for that rejection was the cross. That is why we have Lent. Against the pressure to be a messiah of force, Jesus accepted his mission from his Father: to be the Messiah of enduring love. For fidelity to this mission, he was executed.

If this rejection of Christ had happened only that one time in Jerusalem, it would be sufficient reason for us to spend the time of Lent in penance and prayer, expressing repentance and sorrow for what our Beloved suffered. However, the rejection has happened many times over since that Friday in Jerusalem. The same rejection still exists in our lives today. Every time we choose the way of power and force over the way of powerlessness and surrender, we are rejecting Christ. Every time we choose the way of control and violence over the way of freedom and nonviolence, we are rejecting Christ. Every time we choose bitterness and revenge over forgiveness and compassion, we are rejecting Christ.

Lent is the time for us to reflect on the life and message, the passion and death of Jesus Christ. The first resolution we need to make is a concrete decision about how we are going to allow this Christ the opportunity to speak to us, to teach us, to convert us.

The obvious place to begin to hear Christ is in his words. After praying for hearts and spirits open to the word of God, we can read the Bible every day. It isn't necessary to read pages and pages at a time. Sometimes just a few words or a story is enough. It is good to read the word of God as if for the first time, allowing the strength and power of the word to penetrate us like a two-edged sword. Christ will speak to us through the gospel.

Reading the inspired words of God leads us to pray over them. We can pray every day. Christ will speak to us through prayer. Daily Mass is probably the most common form of Lenten prayer. How good to gather in the morning before work or a busy day to be with other people of God as we partake of mystery. Anytime of the year liturgy is the greatest prayer because it is the prayer of Christ, but during this season it focuses us as nothing else can. As we contemplate the sacrifice of Christ for us, we are present to the reality of that sacrifice. We share in it; we make it our own.

Lenten prayer continues to have its effect in our lives far beyond the actual times of prayer. As we pray with the nonviolent Lamb of God, we open ourselves to become the nonviolent Lamb of God. We become willing to let mercy replace justice, compassion replace hatred. We become open to the possibility of conversion. We become open to the truth of God in our lives.

Prayer is not magic that works automatically with the saying of words; it is an experience of God, of truth. The validity of our Lenten prayer must be measured by the manner in which we live our daily lives. Our patience with our children, spouses, and friends will be the fruit of truthful prayer. Our refusal to take part in any violence in our homes or in society will be the fruit of truthful prayer. Our honesty and tolerance of differences in our workplaces and businesses will be the fruit of truthful prayer.

Lent calls for a denial of sin and all its effects. Yes, it can be a good thing to do some form of physical penance such as fasting or abstinence, but it is a far better thing to live in a manner consistent with the ethic of Christ. We look at "what" could change in our daily lives, but only if we keep focused on "who" we are imitating. All the things we give up are the reminders of the conversion Christ is offering us.

To abstain from alcohol reminds us of our refusal to surrender our consciences to any false drug. To refrain from eating candy or sweets reminds us of our need to refrain from greed. To quit smoking during Lent reminds us that our bodies are the temples of God. To give up watching movies that glorify sexual and physical violence reminds us that every other human being is also a temple of God and deserves to be treated as such.

Above all else, Lent can be the time when the healing warmth of the Son of God reaches into our hearts to bring light, just as the spring days bring the lengthening rays of each day's sun into our winter-weary lives.

Jesus, suffering servant of God, be here among us.

Reflection

1. Who is Jesus Christ for me this Lent?

2. Jesus Christ was not accepted. How do I feel about this fact? What decisions will I make because of it? Are there ways I am not accepted because I am a Christian?

3. What will my Lenten prayer be? How will it be seen in the way I live? What will my Lenten penance be? How will it foster my living like Christ?

ARCHBISHOP OSCAR ROMERO

Here let us stand, close by the cathedral. Here let us wait.
Are we drawn by danger? Is it the knowledge of safety that
    draws our feet
Towards the cathedral? What danger can be
For us, the poor, the poor women of Canterbury? What
    tribulation
With which we are not already familiar? There is no danger
For us, and there is no safety in the cathedral. Some pres-
    age of an act
Which our eyes are compelled to witness, has forced our
    feet
Towards the cathedral. We are forced to bear witness.[6]

An unfinished cathedral stands in the plaza in San Salvador
in mute testimony to the archbishop who refused to complete
it as long as his people were poorly housed and hungry. Archbishop Oscar Romero in death left behind, not a façade of
marble and gold, but a monument of commitment to God
and to justice for the people of God, a commitment that cost
him his life. A bullet from the gun of a hooded assassin, who
was standing in the back of the small chapel next to the cathedral, penetrated the heart of this faithful priest while he was
offering the Eucharist on March 24, 1980. From that day on,
the people of El Salvador have claimed their archbishop as
a saint. The lengthy and costly process of official canoniza-

tion is as unnecessary to Salvadorans as marble in their cathedral.

Who was this man so well known and loved after only three years as archbishop? Oscar Romero throughout most of his life was intense and anxious. He entered the seminary at the age of thirteen and studied hard for the priesthood. He was intelligent and was sent to Rome to get a doctorate, an experience that left him with a great love for the Church of Rome. With an instinct for perfection, he often suffered from scrupulosity. His colleagues sometimes found him demanding and unapproachable, a conservative legalist. Yet, just prior to his death he was known and loved by every poor person in El Salvador. The army called him a revolutionary; The poor called him their voice. To those who said Archbishop Romero had changed, he responded that circumstances had changed.

Perhaps both realities were true. Circumstances had changed and the archbishop changed to respond to them. Archbishop Romero spent his life searching for the will of God, and God used him in a time of great crisis when the will of God was clearly in opposition to the will of the state and the military. To stand for God was to risk persecution by the state. Archbishop Romero and many Salvadorans stood for God.

Only three weeks after Romero's installation as archbishop of San Salvador, Fr. Rutilio Grande, one of his pastors, was murdered along with two parishioners—an old man and a young boy. Archbishop Romero spoke out fearlessly against the injustice and brutality. He held their wake in the cathedral and broadcast their funeral over the radio, urging all the people to resist such bloody force and intimidation.

With this tragedy began the weekly radio sessions of the Archbishop. Speaking fearlessly even after death threats, Archbishop Romero encouraged his people to work for justice and to demand their human rights. He became the "voice of the poor."

Daily Eucharist and meditation, frequent confession, the rosary, regularly scheduled retreat days, and acts of penance

formed and sustained this courageous spokesman of the oppressed. By being faithful to God through a spirituality rooted
in prayer and surrender, he was led beyond legalism to freedom. He knew that the Church did not belong to the priests
and bishops alone but to all the people of God.

Two weeks before he was assassinated, Archbishop
Romero said: "You can tell them, if they succeed in killing
me, that I pardon and bless those who do it. But I wish that
they would realize that they are wasting their time. A bishop
may die, but the Church of God, which is the people, will
never die." If the Church cannot be killed, then neither can
the voice of the faithful prophet of the Church. It echoes far
beyond El Salvador, and we are all blessed because of it.

With his life and death, Archbishop Romero lived the
words T. S. Eliot put on the lips of another archbishop,
Thomas Becket, just before his death in the cathedral:

> Unbar the doors! throw open the doors!
> I will not have the house of prayer, the church of Christ,
> The sanctuary, turned into a fortress.
> The Church shall protect her own, in her own way, not
> As oak and stone; stone and oak decay,
> Give no stay, but the Church shall endure.
> The church shall be open, even to our enemies. Open the
> door![7]

May the soul of Archbishop Romero and the souls of all the
faithful peacemakers who have suffered persecution for
justice's sake rest in peace. Amen.

Jesus, friend of the poor, be here among us.

Reflection

1. Do I know the story of Archbishop Romero and the
recent history of his people in El Salvador? Is it important
that I learn about him?

2. Is there any way in my life that I am a voice for the poor? Does my baptism require me to be this voice?

3. "The church shall be open, even to our enemies. Unbar the doors." How can we help open the doors of our parish to our enemies?

March 25

THE ANNUNCIATION[8]

The most passionate act of womanly love the world has ever known took place in Galilee two thousand years ago when a young woman of childbearing age freely surrendered her entire being, every future moment of her life to God. This abandonment brought forth a child, a man-God whose presence has forever changed the face of the earth.

Mary, in the intimacy and the totality of this great act of freedom, opened herself not only to her God but also to all the people of God—to all of us. Once and for all, Mary entered into the plan of salvation as no one else ever has.

Mary, as a faithful Hebrew woman, knew well the salvation history of her people. She knew the stories of the good and the bad. She knew the beauty of creation and the presence of evil. From the time angels chose not to worship God and refused to acknowledge God as God, evil has existed. Along with the existence of sin, however, has been the promise of redemption. God never left humanity without hope. For years God formed covenants and re-formed them after they were broken. God spoke to admonish, to encourage, to instruct. God spoke through generations of holy men and women. And finally, when the fullness of time had arrived, God chose to speak through Jesus Christ.

With the greatest risk, God let this divine intervention wait upon the word of a virgin daughter of Israel. God allowed the coming of Christ to depend upon the response of a creature of God. God asked Mary if she would be the mother of God. Mary had been chosen and prepared, kept free of any ancestral tendency to sin. She had been formed in the covenants of Yahweh. Desirous of the coming of the Messiah, she had learned to kneel before Yahweh, to worship, to find joy and hope in her God. Her whole being grew in anticipation of Yahweh to come; her heart was eager for her God. This receptivity was the essence of her virginity. She became the virgin mother of God because she allowed the power of God to overshadow her and the presence of God to fill her.

This is our model for virginity. To understand the yes that Mary spoke at the annunciation, we have to see her clearly as virgin. To repeat that yes in our own lives, we have to see ourselves just as clearly as virgins. Virginity is a reality that is poorly understood today. Virginity, in its narrowest sense, can be applied to a person, male or female, who has not had sexual intercourse. The virginity of Mary calls us to far more than that. In her virginity, Mary gives us the model for our own.

Virginity is unconsummated receptivity and openness to God working with us and through us. It is total surrender to the loved one in advance, the abandonment of all defenses and reserves in the presence of the beloved. It is the naked willingness to take on a destiny utterly contrary to the culture of the day. It is the commitment to accept the seed of God in order to give the life of Christ to the world. Once we accept the seed, we are committed to nourishing it. Christ will grow in us and be born of us, and we will be responsible for him from that moment on.

This is the grace of virginity we received with our baptism, the grace to open ourselves to Christ in unrestricted anticipation, the grace that is ours whether we are male or female, married or single, religious or lay. This is the grace of virginity that calls us to passionate single-heartedness, all-consuming and all-embracing. This is the grace of virginity that inflamed Mary.

To the beauty of such receptive virginity God offered motherhood, an inconceivable reality to which Mary freely assented. With that single yes, Mary conceived the Savior and Redeemer of the world. As no one else ever could, Mary, in the ecstasy of her surrendered virginity, embodied the Word of God. The one whom the universe could not contain rested within her womb. Mary became responsible for the child of her womb. She became responsible for all his hopes and dreams as he grew. She became responsible for all the children of God for whom he would give his life. We owe Mary love because it is through her that we have Christ, the Savior of the world.

On this Feast of the Annunciation we pray with Mary that we may also surrender to the passion of God for the salvation of the world. Our vocation is the same as Mary's. By baptism we are called to bring Christ into our world. To do this as Mary did, we must stand vulnerable before God and freely abandon all that we have been and are and ever will be. Total love is the only appropriate response to Total Love.

Jesus, desire of virgins, be here among us.

Reflection

1. Do I think of Mary as a passionate, determined woman? How does this idea of Mary affect my life?

2. Virginity is "total surrender to the loved one in advance." What does this mean to me?

3. I stand in the presence of God. I allow God to ask me to accept the responsibility of giving Christ to the world. What is my response?

Good Friday

DEATH PENALTY

News Bulletin: Jerusalem, A.D. 33, Friday after Passover

Jesus, originally from Nazareth, was executed today after a speedy trial following his arrest on Thursday evening. He was found guilty of insurrection. The death penalty was imposed, and he was crucified about noon. He was the son of Mary, also from Nazareth, and Joseph, who is deceased. His mother witnessed his death. He is reported to have many followers from the Galilee area, but none were available for comment.

Unexplained tremors shook Jerusalem at 3 p.m. yesterday afternoon, causing damage to the Temple and accompanied by a blackout period. Authorities are still investigating the unusual occurrences.

News Bulletin: Mississippi, September 2, 1983

Jimmy Lee Gray was executed today by the state of Mississippi by lethal gas. After the cyanide gas rose from the floor, Jimmy Lee had convulsions for eight minutes and gasped for breath. He struck his head repeatedly on the pole behind him.

News Bulletin: Texas, March 14, 1984

James Autry was executed today by the state of Texas by lethal injection. Taking at least ten minutes to die, James complained of the pain and was conscious until the end.

News Bulletin: Indiana, October 16, 1985

William Vandiver was executed today by the state of Indiana by electrocution. William took five charges of electricity over a seventeen-minute period before he died.

———————————

Jesus Christ was a victim of capital punishment. Everything that was done to Jesus was legal. Does that mean that his executioners and the people who supported the killing were morally free of any responsibility for the death of Jesus?

The death penalty is legal in many states in our country. Does that mean that Catholics are free of any moral responsibility for the homicide justified by the state? As members of the Catholic Church, we are called to be faithful to the teachings of the Church. As we try to be faithful in protecting the life of the unborn, so also must we be faithful in protecting the life of those already born.

Many Catholics are familiar with the Church's teachings on abortion. Far fewer are aware of its teachings on capital punishment. Put most simply, this means that we as Church have not taught well.

Our bishops have spoken clearly and consistently against the death penalty since 1974. In 1980 they issued their most extensive and thorough statement on this *(U.S. Bishops' Statement on Capital Punishment)*. In addition to this, local bishops in over twenty-three states have issued statements on this subject.[9]

The rationale behind the bishops' condemnation of the death penalty is consistent with their stand on pro-life issues in general: life is given by God, and only God has the right to judge when it should end. We are not God and have no right to take life under any circumstances. We are children of God and followers of the Christ, who told us to love our enemies.

Capital punishment cannot be reconciled with love of enemies. It cannot be reconciled with respect for life. Many Catholics do not believe this. We need to be converted and educated and encouraged to follow the courageous words of Christ. We need to hear in our churches the words of our bishops against capital punishment as clearly as we have heard their words against abortion.

The death penalty needs to be faced with honesty, and the myths surrounding it exposed. The United States, Russia, China, Nigeria, Iran, Iraq, Bangladesh, and South Africa are the major countries that currently use the death penalty. Only four countries execute juveniles: Iran, Iraq, Bangladesh, and the United States.

In practice, the death penalty is discriminatory against the poor and racial minorities. It is more expensive than life imprisonment. Abolition of the death penalty could save the state of California $91 million per year. In Florida an execution costs $3.2 million, while forty years in prison costs $516,000. Six mentally handicapped persons have been executed since 1984. In this century twenty-three executed persons were later shown to be innocent. One hundred sixteen persons sentenced to death were found innocent before execution.[10]

No study has ever shown the death penalty to be a deterrent to crime. On the contrary, abolition of the death penalty might begin to break the cycle of violence. It would express our belief in the worth of each person as created by God and redeemed from sin at the price of Jesus' blood.

One day in Galilee, at the stoning of a woman taken in adultery, Jesus was asked his opinion of the death penalty. It was the law that she be stoned. Jesus addressed the crowd, "Let anyone among you who is without sin be the first to throw a stone at her" (John 8:7). No one in the crowd con-

demned her, nor did Jesus condemn her. Neither can we condemn her or anyone else who has sinned.

On Good Friday we venerate the image of our crucified
Lord. It is a good day to repent of our share in today's crucifix-
ions and to pray for one another that we turn from this evil.

Jesus, rejected Messiah, be here among us.

Reflection

1. Does my state or country have the death penalty? When
was the last execution? How many convicted men and women
are on death row? What is my responsibility in this matter?

2. I kneel in front of the crucifix in the presence of Jesus.
What is his response to evil? What is mine?

3. Jesus says, "Let anyone among you who is without
sin be the first to throw a stone at her." When do I pick up
the first stone? What must I do in my life to put down the
stone?

APRIL TO JUNE:
INTRODUCTION

Jesus, risen Lord, raise us to new life.

April

Every Gospel scene of the resurrected Jesus begins with a word of peace. During this Easter Season we dare to believe in resurrection, in the triumph of love over hate, of peace over violence. Belief implies action. If we believe in the power of love, we will act in the power of love. *Jesus, Lord of peace, raise us to new life.*

As Easter is a season, not just a day, it gives us the opportunity to enter into the mystery of resurrection as a process, not a completed event. Jesus' resurrection in Jerusalem is completed, but our share in that rising to new life is ongoing. The power of the resurrection is that sin has been conquered, forgiveness and mercy have replaced guilt and punishment. To be Easter people, we must also enter into the process of forgiveness. Mercy is the mark of the Christian, not retribution. *Jesus, forgiver of sins, raise us to new life.*

The act of forgiveness does not take away the pain we feel as a result of another's sin. Our wounds endure beyond our choice to forgive. Even here we believe in the grace of redemption, especially for those who have left the impact of hate on us. We believe that nothing and no one is beyond the power of God's healing touch. In our woundedness we speak mercy, and mercy speaks hope to us. *Jesus, healer of wounds, raise us to new life.*

In the resurrection appearances of Jesus, he constantly encourages his disciples not to fear. There is no place for fear in the Christian life, not because we manipulate our emotions, but because we trust our risen Lord. We choose to trust rather than to fear. We choose to let God protect us rather than defend ourselves. *Jesus, liberator from fear, raise us to new life.*

May

Our responsibility to be Christians must show in every aspect of our lives. Through Jesus' resurrection all life on earth has been changed. We share in this change when our lives speak of resurrection and love. We share in this change when our lives speak justice and peace. Most of us spend a large part of our time at work, so it is at work that we must reflect the ways of the risen Christ. Society's standards of business are not our standards. We ask Joseph the Worker to intercede for us in this difficult task of keeping Christ in the marketplace. *Jesus, stepson of Joseph, raise us to new life.*

As Joseph can help us in the marketplace, Mary can guide us through the intricacies of love in the home. Mothers are entrusted by God with the fragile lives of their children. We are all responsible for all the children, so this day for mothers is a day for all. *Jesus, nurturer of children, raise us to new life.*

It is hard to focus simultaneously on mothers who nurture children and on wars that destroy children. Yet we do that. We gather our children together, buy them little flags and hot dogs, and watch a parade of soldiers with guns and tanks. We clap and wave and cheer at the representatives of an industry whose purpose is to destroy and kill. We are the body of Christ. Those whom we kill in war are the body of Christ. We desperately need the feast of the Body and Blood of Christ at this time to counter the military message of Memorial Day. *Jesus, bread of life, raise us to new life.*

What we celebrate in the Feast of the Visitation also contradicts what we are saying when we celebrate military victories. Mary visits Elizabeth, a simple act of human kindness. Out of this meeting comes the *Magnificat,* Mary's song of praise. "My soul magnifies the Lord, and my spirit rejoices in God my Savior" (Luke 1:46-47).

If we wish it, out of our celebration of this meeting can come our song of praise as well. What the Visitation tells us is that we are created to be beings of praise, expressing the love of God. What military celebrations tell us is that we are created to be beings of power, expressing the supremacy of the state. We are not created to substitute military supremacy for surrender to God or to trade trust in the Father for dependency upon arms. We are created to be beings of praise. In this creation we rejoice. *Jesus, joy of the poor in spirit, raise us to new life.*

June

Resurrection requires resistance. As we refuse to cooperate in the celebration of military victories, so we refuse to cooperate in the glorification of political power in sacred places. Whenever we hang a national flag in the sanctuary of a church, we are mixing the glory of God with the glory of the state. In two thousand years of Christianity that mix hasn't worked for the good of the Church; it has only clouded the issues and allowed the Church to be the puppet of the state. Flag Day is a national holiday, not a religious feast. Christianity cannot be limited by national boundaries. *Jesus, protector of all people, raise us to new life.*

Decisions to follow the way of Christ are made both individually and communally. The parades are held because they are supported by a local community of people; the flags are kept in churches because the parish communities want them. This influence of the community is also critical to the development of our children's faith. As we graduate children from our schools, we should use the occasion to examine our efforts at educating them in the faith. *Jesus, heart of Christian communities, raise us to new life.*

Like graduations, marriages are community affairs. A man and a woman in the presence of a community, a faith community for some, vow mutual fidelity before God. Marriage is a wonderful expression of the willingness of the human heart to be open and vulnerable to another. There is cause for celebration and there is cause for prayer, on the day of the marriage and on every day after it. *Jesus, bond of fidelity, raise us to new life.*

We end our resurrection reflections while touching the beauty of the rose. Opening itself to the sun's rays, the rose reveals all its inner beauty, holding nothing back. Mary teaches us to open ourselves to her Son's warmth, holding nothing back. The wonder is that the Son also opens himself, holding nothing back. In this mutual opening, inner beauty of creature becomes one with infinite beauty of Creator. *Jesus, arouser of mystics, raise us to new life.*

EASTER:
MARY OF THE RESURRECTION

Jesus Christ rose from the dead three days after his execution in Jerusalem. For forty days he went among his friends and followers, encouraging them and teaching them. He met his disciples in gardens and at seasides, in upper rooms and on the roads. He met them when they were alone and when they were together. He prayed with them and taught them. He prepared fish for them and fed them Eucharist.

One thing remained constant in all the different appearances. Every Gospel scene of the resurrected Jesus begins with a word of peace. The call of the resurrection is a call to peace. We turn to Mary during this Easter Season to help us understand this call. As Mary was faithful to Christ's death, so was she faithful to his resurrection. We come to ask Mary to form us into people of the resurrection whose words, like Christ's, are words of peace and whose lives, like Christ's, are lives of peace.

The Quakers and Mennonites and Church of the Brethren are some of the sects usually considered peace Churches. Considering the example and words of Jesus Christ, why is it that all Christian Churches are not considered peace Churches?

If we based our beliefs on the life and message of Jesus, as we claim to do, there would be no doubt that we are a peace Church. Every act and every word of Jesus were acts and words of peace. He clearly told us to love one another, even our enemies; he told us to forgive seventy times seven times. He reached out to all peoples; none were excluded from his presence or his compassionate, healing love. He died loving his persecutors. And when he rose from the dead, his greeting to his apostles was "Peace be with you" (Luke 24:36).

To understand this mission to be peacemakers, we go to Mary. We go to her because she was present at Bethlehem when the Word of God took flesh to live among us as the Prince of Peace, and because she was present on Calvary when the Word of God gave up his flesh to make peace with God for us. Mary enters our lives and our hearts, not as a priceless statue on a pedestal, but as a woman who was entrusted with being the first and most faithful disciple of Christ, the Man of Peace.[11]

Our mission to make peace is to be a reflection of Christ's mission. Christ's mission was to praise and glorify God and to proclaim the truth in peace. Our mission is to praise and glorify God and to proclaim the truth in peace. Our mission is not to judge or condemn those who contribute to violence, injustice, and oppression. Our mission is not even to insist on converting them. Judgment and conversion are ultimately the work of God alone. Our task is to be true to Christ's message of love and mercy, to witness to peace and truth with our lives, to give our lives in love for others.

If we wish to be sharers in Christ's work of peace, then we do what he did—open our arms in love on the cross in abandonment to the will of God for the love of God's people. This tremendous responsibility is the duty of every baptized person.

The call to the mission of peacemaking is a call for all Christians, not only for a few exceptional prophets. The people of God who try to live daily the call to love of enemies are not on the fringe of the Christian message—they are at the center of it. Such love is the heart of Christ's life and death.

Christ's mother understood this, and we need her to guide us into this same understanding. As peacemakers, we need the guidance of Mary to be faithful to the call to be loving and forgiving as Jesus was. This is not an easy task in a Church that has condoned violence and blessed war for over seventeen hundred years. Mary sustained a Church of trembling apostles after the resurrection, and she will sustain us today. We look at the weakness of our Church and of ourselves, yet we stand firm in the hope of the peace to which we have been called.

Mary, through giving birth to Jesus, participated in the redemption of the world. We also are called to participate in redeeming the world with love. In our day we have the technological ability to destroy the world. We have the psychological ability to destroy countless human lives through personal violence. Our mission is to refuse to participate in such violence and to choose peace in every detail of our lives. Our mission is to choose peace for ourselves and for all the people of God.

Jesus gave us this peace at the cost of his life. Mary lived through every word of his gospel of peace with her life. To live the gospel of Jesus, we need his presence and the presence of his Mother. We need to pray with Mary and to stay with her as we surrender ourselves to the risen Lord of Peace.

Jesus, Lord of peace, raise us to new life.

Reflection

1. Why aren't Catholic Churches considered peace churches?

2. What did Christ's life say about his message of peace? What did his death say? What does my life say about peace?

3. What does it mean to believe in resurrection? How can Mary help us embrace this reality?

RESURRECTION FROM SIN: CONFESSION

The Easter Season carries with it many images. Spring is the most common. These days of April, with their longer periods of daylight, make sun-watchers of all of us. Even if winter seems to be still lingering with a cold wind or a late snowstorm, something in us is conscious of spring. We are able to tease warmth out of any day. Storm windows are being taken down, heavy winter coats and boots are ready to be stored away, and seedlings are begun in the protection of a window box in a sunny place. The breeze even smells different as newly awakened trees and plants put forth their buds.

Liturgically we have celebrated new life in the resurrection of Jesus. The Lamb of God has taken away the sin of the world. No matter how ugly and hateful we may feel, we have been redeemed. The heavy coat of sin and the boots of hate that slow us down we can put aside forever. It is the spring of faith; we can walk unencumbered and free in the light of Christ who has assumed our burdens.

As wondrous as resurrection from sin and death is, even this will not be forced upon us. Always our God insists that we be free to choose. We are offered freedom from sin through the power of the resurrection of Jesus. We are offered forgiveness for our sins and healing for the sin of the world.

There is no greater way to appreciate this season than to celebrate it with the sacrament of reconciliation. Confession is an experience of forgiveness, a share in the forgiveness

Christ brought about on Calvary. It is not a sacrament that feeds guilt. It is sorrow, not guilt, that brings us to it.

A first-grade child made the comment: "Sometimes we can say no to God." It is that simple. There are times in our lives when we turn from God and from one another. We say no to the works of mercy and love, and we say yes to hatred or evil. The freedom of our choice varies. There are times when weakness and fear prevent us from doing the good we ought to do; there are times when greed or injured pride cause us to willingly hurt ourselves or others. These are the times we say no to God and to life; these are the times we sin.

Because of Christ's presence among us, the last word does not have to be that of sin, no matter how unforgivable we may believe it to be. To believe in resurrection is to believe that love conquers all. To live this belief is to bear witness to the enduring power of love.

The sacrament of reconciliation gives us the opportunity to say with words that we are sorry that we have offended God, sorry that we have hurt ourselves and that we have hurt others. The sacrament allows us the experience of receiving forgiveness and of becoming a forgiving person.

Calvary doesn't end when we walk away from the crucifixion. Confession doesn't end when we walk away from the encounter with the priest. That is the beginning. We have been given a penance, a symbol of conversion. Outside the confessional we pray our penance, but even that is not the end of the reconciliation. Now we are responsible for fidelity to that fragile conversion which has begun again in us through the grace of God and the grace of the sacrament.

Every gift from God carries its own responsibility. God's gifts are free, but they draw us into the experience of love and the need for response. With this sacrament we are drawn into the process of forgiveness. And forgiveness is a process, not a feeling. To enter into this process is to enter into continual conversion. Forgiveness requires faith, effort, and determination. We acknowledge our need for forgiveness, we believe that God forgives us, and we accept the obligation to forgive others. Throughout our lives we live this cycle of forgiveness as a never-ending process.

Terry Anderson, the American hostage who was held the longest and was the last to be released in Lebanon, came home determined to forgive. He had spent seven years in captivity. Terry accepted his responsibility as a Christian to forgive. "Forgiveness," he said, "is not a thing that we just do, and then it's done. It's a process, a hard one, that needs to be worked at every day. But I have come to believe most strongly in Christ's simple dictum—if I wish to be forgiven my so many sins, I have to forgive. I'm not yet a good Christian, but I'm trying."[12]

Terry Anderson left seven years of captivity without the burden of revenge. This season we can lay down the burden of darkness and accept the new light of Easter in Christ. At the same time that we accept the freedom offered us by Christ, we can bestow on others the light of our forgiveness, so that their burden of darkness can also be lifted.

No tomb could contain Jesus. We are not consigned to the tomb of sin, and we should not keep others in the tomb of their mistakes. In Jesus the light of resurrection frees our bodies and spirits, and we rise again and again and again in witness to enduring love.

Jesus, forgiver of sins, raise us to new life.

Reflection

1. What is the difference between sorrow and guilt? Which do I choose?

2. Have I said no to God? What is my response to this?

3. When was the last time I took advantage of the sacrament of reconciliation? How do I help others by this sacrament?

RESURRECTION FROM WOUNDEDNESS: HEALING OF MEMORIES

As the sacrament of reconciliation is the healing for our sins, belief in the resurrection of Christ is the healing for the woundedness we have suffered as a result of others' sins. Neglect, abuse, violence, physical and emotional deprivation, tragedies or illness have left most of us wounded in one way or another.

To believe in the resurrection means that we cannot stop at our wounds. If we did, it would give our woundedness control over our lives. We are more free than that. Our wounds do not stop our response to God, which is the only thing that matters.

If this seems cruel or touched with a denial of reality, compare emotional woundedness with physical handicaps. People with paralyzed legs cannot run a marathon race. They may participate as wheelchair contestants but they cannot run. Still, their physical handicaps do not make them less pleasing to God. There is no lack of wholeness in these people in the eyes of God. There is no limit on their ability to love and share in the redemption of the world.

What we see so clearly on the level of physical handicaps is not always as obvious on the emotional level. Because of environment, background, personal life experiences, deprivation, illness, genetic make-up, and thousands of other factors that go into our emotional health, we all bear handicaps, some more noticeable than others.

In our lives we work to lessen the damaging effects of emotional handicaps as we work to lessen the damaging effects of physical handicaps. God expects us to take advantage of all the ways to health that are available to us. God delights in wholeness—it is the nature of God's Being. But God sees us and rejoices in us while we are still a long way off. Our emotional handicaps are not a barrier to our relationship with God or to our ability to fully live a Christian life. Wounds do not keep us from standing before God and one another in the beauty of our being. Every child of God can proclaim, "My being proclaims the greatness of my God."

Even wounds that have been inflicted on people as children cannot ruin their lives in the sight of God. Children who have suffered physical or emotional abuse carry limitations that are as obvious as an artificial leg, but these children are not limited in responding to love and in love. Even if they have been repeatedly abused sexually, even if they may not be capable of entering into a happy marriage and raising children of their own, still, they are not less able to be loving than children who have been raised in great love and family security. Love may be expressed differently in their lives, but it will not be denied them.

Society's standards are not the standards by which love can be measured, and we cannot allow ourselves to be caught up in such falsehoods. We measure by the standards of Christ, and we owe it to our brothers and sisters to teach them the true standards. We are more than just the product of what has been done to us—we have been formed in the love of Christ. This is our hope. Sharing this hope with others is our responsibility.

To live this way is to live in a deep experience of faith, faith that God created us for wholeness in love, and in love we will be fulfilled. This is faith which believes that nothing that has been done to us, no matter how painful or devastating, can diminish the quality of our love. Unfortunate circumstances and unwanted pain and disappointments can cause us to arm ourselves with bitterness, hatred, and resentments, weapons that are dangerous. We ruthlessly use these weapons on one another sometimes. Yet, how often the problem is not with others but within ourselves. How often the problem is the painful wound of a shattered emotion.

Like the prophet Jeremiah, we risk faith and cry, "Truly this is my punishment, and I must bear it" (Jeremiah 10:19). We are not running from the source of sorrow. We are acknowledging it, but we are also acknowledging the power of God over it.

In the movie *War and Peace,* the final scene depicts this sense of hope in the midst of sorrow. The war is over and Natasha, the beautiful and hopeful heroine, has returned home with what remains of her family. Most of the house has been destroyed   only one wing still stands. Everyone else looks despairingly at the house except Natasha. She delights in the wing that is almost intact. At this moment Pierre, a long-time friend who was abandoned as a child, arrives on crutches, with one side of his body badly wounded. Pierre didn't fight in the war, but he was hurt helping the wounded on the battlefield. Natasha looks at Pierre and says, "You are like this house. You suffer. You show your wounds but you stand."

Woundedness is inherent in the human condition. Redemption is the discovery that the Holy Spirit dwells at the center of our wounds. This gives us the ability to stand before God in our brokenness. We suffer, yet we stand. Our wounds show, yet we stand before God.

We cannot stand before God in the simplicity of our own truth unless we stand before one another in that same simplicity. There is no need to cover our wounds; they are the truth of our being. And they are beautiful because they have been redeemed into the Alleluia chorus of a resurrected community. "My being proclaims the greatness of my God."

Jesus, healer of wounds, raise us to new life.

Reflection

1. What woundedness in my life am I conscious of? Does this woundedness control me? Do I believe that nothing can be a barrier to my response to God?

2. Have I armed myself with bitterness or resentment? Am I willing to allow the healing hope of Christ to remove these defenses?

3. Can I simply stand before God, in my gifts and in my weaknesses, and know that I am loved intimately and unreservedly? Can I pray, ''My being proclaims the greatness of my God''?

RESURRECTION FROM FEAR: FREEDOM OF SPIRIT

"Do not be afraid; I am the first and the last, and the living one. I was dead, and see, I am alive forever and ever" (Revelation 1:17, 18).

"There is no fear in love, but perfect love casts out fear" (1 John 4:18).

Fear is a controlling emotion. It can cause us to do harm and it can prevent us from doing good. It can paralyze us and it can send us into a rage. It can increase our strength and it can weaken us.

When the World Trade Center in New York was bombed, the governor of that state said that the tool of terrorists is fear. They strike at random, trying to leave people in a constant state of uncertainty and fear. A return to normalcy is the only effective way to neutralize terrorists.

If we can try to handle our fears on a human level, how much more can we hope to do with the aid of the Divine? The resurrection of Jesus frees us from fear. It gives us the faith and courage to reject fear. This rejection takes practice. Freedom from fear is not an emotion, it is a choice. It is not a feeling that we simply have or don't have—that comes and goes. Freedom from fear is a choice of faith deeper than our emotions, and our emotions are subject to this choice.

Fear can be controlling. Fear of strangers can keep us from welcoming anyone we don't know. Fear of what our enemies can do to us can keep us from loving them and being open to them. Fear of ridicule can keep us from speaking the truth and standing by our convictions. Fear of social sanctions can force us into rigid patterns of dress and behavior. Fear of our own infidelity can abort commitment. Fear of the violence in the slums of our cities can prevent us from going into them to help the homeless or the destitute. Fear can grip compassionate hearts and prevent them from expressing the love they feel.

St. Francis of Assisi had this experience: he was afraid of lepers. One day he kissed a leper and the fear vanished. It is important to note that the fear vanished after he kissed the leper, not before. Before the fear left him, Francis had to take the risk of loving.

It is not possible for us to assist every homeless person we meet. But it is possible to look at each one of them and think "brother" or "sister." After a while our fear will ebb, and that which took great effort in the beginning will come as naturally to us as a smile to a baby.

There are many people working day after day in the middle of violent neighborhoods. If we want to help there, we can have those who are already there show us the way; we can find support. Fear must not be our excuse. We take the necessary precautions for safety, but we move. After all, men, women, and children are living in those same neighborhoods through which we are afraid to drive. Fear must be replaced by fearlessness.

Fearlessness is a tremendous power. Stories abound of people who have actually disarmed violent aggressors by their lack of fear. Such fearlessness does not come easily. It is the fruit of deliberate acts of kindness toward those we initially fear. Fearlessness is God's challenge to us and God's gift to us; it grows quietly and surely. It is the strength behind nonviolence. Just as fear can lead us to erect defenses, so fearlessness can lead us to dismantle them. It is necessary to be free from fear if we are to stop relying on guns and bombs for protection.

There is a mutuality here in terms of cause and effect. It is necessary to work against fear if we are to try loving our enemies, and it is absolutely necessary to risk loving our enemies if we want to be free of fear. Like St. Francis, we need to risk acts of love before we experience feelings of love. The greatest love we can show others is to believe in their ability to be loving themselves. Even while recognizing the sin that abounds everywhere, we must choose to trust in others' capacity to love, in God's power to gift them with love. It is not through psychological maneuvering that we achieve this fearlessness but by complete trust in God.

Fearlessness requires trust in our enemies. We must be willing to take a chance on their openness to conversion, to risk the possibility of their conversion. We must be willing to stake something on their potential for goodness. We can never decide when someone else is beyond redemption. We are not God.

We learn not to fear when we learn to trust God and the ways of God. We act out of this fearlessness because we know that this God of ours will never abandon us. We may suffer violence, but we will not suffer abandonment by God. This confidence keeps the violence from terrorizing us and keeps us free to concentrate on love rather than defense.

Jesus, liberator from fear, raise us to new life.

Reflection

1. Are there fears in my life that are controlling me? What are they? Can I bring them into the presence of the resurrected Christ? How do I do that? What might happen to my fears if I do that?

2. What enemies am I afraid of? What acts of fearlessness can I choose to work against the fear?

3. What choices have I made this day to express my trust in God?

May 1

ST. JOSEPH THE WORKER

We know little about Joseph, the stepfather of Jesus. We know that Joseph was engaged to Mary when by the Holy Spirit she conceived Jesus in her womb. We know that Joseph was convinced of Mary's virtue, even though he did not understand the mystery of her pregnancy. We know that Joseph listened to angels and paid attention to dreams that God sent.

Joseph was the man chosen by God to care for Jesus and Mary. That fact in itself speaks volumes for the trustworthiness and integrity of the man. Joseph is present in Scripture in all the accounts of Jesus' birth, during the flight into Egypt, and during the ordeal of losing the twelve-year-old Jesus in Jerusalem.

Jesus was known as the son of Joseph the carpenter. Because there is no mention of Joseph during the public life of Jesus, we assume that Joseph died between the finding in the Temple and the time Jesus began his public life.

Joseph lived with God in the person of Jesus, and Joseph loved Jesus as a son—an extraordinary relationship. Joseph was in love with Mary, and Mary was in love with Joseph— an extraordinary relationship. We can only imagine the depths of passion, respect, and love that were shared in this the most holy of families.

We do not need to invent or fantasize about the details of Joseph's life. We know enough from Scripture to reverence him deeply. The devotion to St. Joseph that people have had through the years is well founded. We know that we can count on Joseph for assistance and guidance within our communion of saints.

We celebrate Joseph as husband of Mary and patron of the universal Church on March 19, but on May 1 the Church honors St. Joseph the Worker. This is a good opportunity to reflect upon the gift and responsibility of work and to seek the intercession of Joseph for God's blessing on our work.

A good place to begin is with our own jobs. The first question we need to ask is about the nature of our work: Are we employed in work that is worthy of a Christian? Does our work bear witness to Christ? As Christians we are responsible for being Christ in our society. We cannot be Christ in employment that is in direct contradiction to the message of Christ. No longer is it sufficient to ask: How much is the pay? What are the benefits? What is the location? As Christians we have to ask more, because more is expected of us.

We are called to express divine love through living the works of mercy. Jesus gave us that standard as the one by which our response to him will be measured. Any work inconsistent with the works of mercy is not fitting for a Christian—not just organized crime, prostitution, and other illegal activities, but also employment in the war industry, abortion clinics, or in any work that glorifies sexual or physical violence. There is implicit or explicit cooperation with evil in all these works, and a Christian can never cooperate with evil.

Once we have determined that our work is not inherently supportive of evil, we must look further to see whether justice and integrity are part of the structure of our work. If we are employers, it is our responsibility to make sure we are paying just wages, safeguarding the dignity of each worker, following fair labor practices, and maintaining working conditions appropriate for members of the body of Christ. As Catholic employers, we support the rights of the worker, particularly the right to organize. The Catholic Church has always done this.

If we are employees, we must do our work with enthusiasm, as people conscious of serving the Lord and not just human beings (see Ephesians 6:7). As members of the body of Christ, we do not waste time or material, pilfer, criticize, or complain. As Christians, we do not try to achieve advancement—whether political, social, or economic—at the expense of others.

At the same time we must positively insist on justice and respect in the workplace. A Christian cannot tolerate or accept discrimination of any kind. There will be times when we may be called to risk our own job or even our personal safety to defend the integrity of another. We must take that risk. The call of the Christian in the marketplace is a call to seek truth, to speak truth, and to live truth.

Beyond being a place that ensures basic human rights, the environment of the workplace ought to be such that it positively promotes mutual toleration and respect. Vulgarity, stereotypical comments, sexual harassment, off-color jokes, and humor at the expense of others are not characteristics of a Christian working environment.

Finally, unemployment ought to be the concern of every Christian, not just of those who find themselves actually out of work. Christians are sympathetically aware of what jobless people suffer. Unemployment can cause a loss of self-esteem, destabilize personalities, contribute to the break-up of marriages and families, lead to an increase in domestic violence, and undermine the health and welfare of children.

God has created us to be fruitful, to fill the earth and bring the earth to fullness in Christ. We reach our human fulfillment as we protect and share in the productivity of this fragile earth and all its people. On this day we honor the blessing of work, and we honor a simple man of work, Joseph the Worker.

Jesus, stepson of Joseph, raise us to new life.

Reflection

1. Is my work worthy of a Christian? Does it bear witness to Christ?

2. What impact do my actions have on the environment of my workplace? How do I bring justice to my job? How do I bring mercy and compassion? How do I bring integrity?

3. Do I know anyone who is unemployed? Is there anything I can do to help him or her financially, emotionally, physically, spiritually?

Second Sunday in May

MOTHER'S DAY

God, you have created and nurtured us as a mother, we bless
  you and we give you praise.
Mothers of us all, living here or in eternity, bless our God.
Mothers of healthy, happy children, bless our God.
Mothers of ill or troubled children, bless our God.
Mothers of children who are well fed and well cared for, bless
  our God.
Mothers of abandoned or neglected children, bless our God.
Mothers of loved children, bless our God.
Mothers of abused children, bless our God.
Mothers of hungry children, bless our God.
Mothers of children of freedom, bless our God.
Mothers of children of oppression, bless our God.
Mothers of children who can go to school and learn, bless our
  God.
Mothers whose children have to work at an early age, bless our
  God.
Mothers whose children have disappeared, bless our God.
Mothers of children who have been tortured and murdered,
  bless our God.
Mothers whose children have died young from disease or pov-
  erty, bless our God.
Mothers in exile, bless our God.

Mothers of children who learn to share and care for others, bless our God.

Mothers of children who commit crimes, bless our God.

Mothers of children whose skin is black, bless our God.

Mothers of children whose skin is white, bless our God.

Mothers of children whose skin is red, bless our God.

Mothers of children whose skin is yellow, bless our God.

Mothers of sorrow and pain, bless our God.

Mothers of joy and life, bless our God.

Mothers who are young and frightened, bless our God.

Mothers who are older and tired, bless our God.

Mothers who are happy to be mothers, bless our God.

Mothers who are confused by motherhood, bless our God.

Mothers who have to work and worry about their children being home without them, bless our God.

Mothers who are able to be at home with their children, bless our God.

Mothers who have the support of loving husbands, bless our God.

Mothers who are unmarried, widowed, or divorced, bless our God.

Mothers who are on welfare and long to be free of it, bless our God.

Mothers who live in cities of violence and fear, bless our God.

Mothers in suburbs of isolation and alienation, bless our God.

Mothers who are at home with their God and teach their children to be at home with God, bless our God.

Mothers who feel distant from God and the people of God, bless our God.

Mothers who are battered and abused, bless our God.

Mothers who are loved and respected, bless our God.

Mothers who suffer physical or mental illness, bless our God.

Mothers who enjoy good health, bless our God.

Mothers of war-torn countries, bless our God.

Mothers who enjoy peace, bless our God.

Mothers of the first world and second world and third world, bless our God.

Mothers who choose to give birth in the face of opposition,
bless our God.
Mother of God, Mary most holy, bless our God.
Through all the mothers of our world, all praise and glory to
God, now and forever. Amen.

Jesus, nurturer of children, raise us to new life.

Reflection

1. As I pray this litany, what moves me? How will I act
on this?

2. Do I know mothers who need support? What will be
my response?

3. Regardless of my sex or vocation, how do I care for,
nourish, and protect the body of Christ?

MEMORIAL DAY AND CORPUS CHRISTI

On Memorial Day weekend, parades and celebrations honor men and women who have served in the military. By association, this day glorifies the use of violence to achieve desired ends, whether noble or otherwise. Depending on the date of Easter, Memorial Day coincides with or falls close to the weekend when we celebrate the Feast of Corpus Christi, now called the Feast of the Body and Blood of Christ. But there is an immeasurable degree of difference between the message of Memorial Day and the message of the Body and Blood of Christ.

The body of Christ is a body given in love for all people, regardless of race, color, nationality, or income. It is a body given in flesh and blood for friend and enemy alike. It is a body given without resistance to death so that we might live. It is a body given in love so that we also might live in love.

To love as Christ loved, which is what we are called to do, we reverently look at him on Calvary as he offers himself to the Father for our sake. An innocent man takes upon himself the burden of evil so that by his suffering all might be free. Christ dies equally for those who stand by the cross and for those who nail him to it.

This same body of Christ is given to us under the form of bread and wine so that we may taste it as food and experience it as love. In the Eucharistic celebration we remember the body of Christ blessed, broken, and given to us on the cross. In the breaking of the bread at Eucharist, we remem-

ber and celebrate the depth of Christ's love and forgiveness
for us, and we share it with one another. Because of the sacrament of Christ's body and blood, every day is a Memorial
Day calling us to love one another.

The bread of Christ is the body of Christ, blessed, broken, and given. The life-stance of the Christian is a surrender
of self into the hands of Christ to be blessed, broken, and given
to others for their nourishment. It is a commitment that simple
and that total.

The control is in the hands of Jesus, not our own. The
blessing is in the hands of Jesus, not our own. The breaking
also will be in the hands of Jesus. No matter what anyone
does to our bodies or our minds, no one can take us from
the hands of Jesus.

From those hands we will be given, as he was, for the
redemption of the world. We don't model our surrender on
that of Jesus—we unite with it. Ours is not a separate sacrifice added to Christ's. Nothing needs to be added to the sacrifice of Jesus Christ; his sacrifice was sufficient to redeem
the world and all its people.

But to make the sacrifice of Jesus present in our age and
time, we long to share in his sacrifice, and Jesus allows us
to share in it. Because we love Jesus, we long to be with him;
we long to share his pain and his glory. As we abandon ourselves to his enticing love, zeal to spread this word of love
propels us toward others. It isn't enough that we have recognized him; we want others to recognize him also. The more
we surrender to him, the more we can be given to nourish
others. We trust our God that we will be given. Christ will
allow us to feed one another.

In our day we do not lack examples of those who have
fed the rest of us. The lives of today's saints are being written in the daily newspapers. Some names are familiar to us,
some are unknown. But they are all the body of Christ, and
so are we. When they feed and nourish us, Christ is fed and
nourished. When they suffer and are broken, Christ suffers
and is broken.

We cannot change the way Christ chose to be part of us. We can accept it or not, but we cannot deny his way of salvation. He chose to use love, not force; he chose to die rather than to kill. If we desire union with him, we must necessarily desire to be united with him in using the same methods he used.

This is the prayer of the Christian: to be united with Christ in his life and in his way of giving life. This must be our prayer if we wish to be one with Jesus for the nourishment of our brothers and sisters, including those who hate us. It is this that we need to remember. It is this that we need to commemorate on Memorial Day.

It is good to remember the dead, especially those who have died in the violence of war, but our remembrance must be consistent with Christ's remembrance. Christ told us how to remember him: "Do this in memory of me." When we remember those who have died in war, we pray in sorrow for the loss of life and the failure of Christians to love one another. We do not celebrate victories, we mourn battles. In war Christ suffers and dies in our brothers and sisters. We suffer their pain, and we remember them when we gather to celebrate Christ's triumph over pain and hatred.

For those who celebrate the body and blood of Christ, for those who celebrate the love of Christ for his people, every day is a memorial day.

Jesus, Bread of Life, raise us to new life.

Reflection

1. Do I participate in or attend parades that glorify military power? What would Christ do with regard to such parades?

2. Do I believe that I receive the body and blood of Christ in Communion? Do I believe that others receive the body and blood of Christ? What does this shared reception of Christ say about our relationship with one another?

3. Is Christ nourishment to me? Am I nourishment to others? How do I express both of these?

May 31

THE VISITATION

After the angel Gabriel told Mary that her cousin Elizabeth was six months pregnant, Mary traveled to help Elizabeth and to be helped by her. Two women preparing for birth, two women intimately involved in preparing for the Messiah meet in the hills of Judea. Elizabeth greets Mary as the mother of her Lord; Elizabeth's child leaps for joy in his mother's womb.

In response to Elizabeth's greeting, words of praise burst from Mary, words of unbounded hope and unbridled enthusiasm. We listen in wonder to Mary's faith and happiness in the prayer that has come down to us as the *Magnificat* (see Luke 1:46-55). This prayer is not only Mary's prayer; it is the prayer of all Christians. It is both call and response, both praise and challenge. It is the cry of one who is loving and being loved at the same time.

"My soul magnifies the Lord, and my spirit rejoices in God my Savior." Mary is in love. She is experiencing the greatest of all human emotions. While carrying within herself the great High Priest, Mary is already living her own call to priesthood: a call to gather the people of God together in a community of love.

We also are baptized into the priesthood of Christ and called by love to be abandoned to God and other people in love. In the mystery of surrendering ourselves to that love, we become more whole and fulfilled than if we tried to hold back from abandonment. Love makes us confident and free, beyond our own emotional and psychological ability to bring it about.

The *Magnificat* is the prayer of the rejoicing heart. Those who are in pain need to pray this prayer. It is the prayer especially of those whose only source of joy and hope is Christ. It is the prayer for the weak and helpless who allow themselves to be absorbed into the strength of God. It is the prayer of any who have been abandoned or abused. No one has a better right than they to cry out: "All generations will call me blessed; for the Mighty One has done great things for me."

When we pray the *Magnificat,* we do not deny woundedness, deprivation, and pain. We acknowledge emotional traumas and scars, but these are not barriers to fulfillment. Faith lets us see beyond our losses. No matter what has been done to us or not done for us, we can never be without the Spirit of God, who prays in us with words deeper than our understanding, giving us hearts able to rejoice in God.

Those who suffer abuse experience degradation because others have not treated them with dignity and respect. Those who suffer abuse do not feel blessed and cannot imagine that generations will proclaim their worth. The *Magnificat* reflects the truth of God, which is that all people were created by God as beings of praise and beauty. Abuse is the falsehood. The *Magnificat* is the cry of truth against the lie of abuse. The truth is that those who have suffered at the hands of others were created by God to be blessed and to be recognized as such. All generations will call them blessed. If some of God's children have not been treated in a loving way, it is not because they do not deserve to be; it is because there is hatred in this world.

As people of faith, we believe that all the hatred and abuse and neglect among the fragile people of this earth are not stronger than the infinite love of God revealed in Jesus Christ. When we pray the *Magnificat,* we express our faith in the primacy of love. Those who have suffered most have earned the right to pray this prayer the most.

Even when feelings cannot match choices, when despair and anger are trying to control us, we must keep on proclaiming, "The Mighty One has done great things for me." It is God's holiness that we share in, and no person or event can ever diminish or block that holiness. Mercy and strength will be given us; we will be raised up from our pain, and our hunger for love will be satisfied. Mercy is promised for all generations.

As the redeemed people of God, we remember this promise of mercy. In remembering we become people who receive mercy and people who give mercy. We become people who are no longer helpless in the face of human tragedy. We cannot change what hate has done, but we can redeem it with love.

In the official Evening Prayer of the Church, those participating stand for the recitation of the *Magnificat*. And whenever we pray that prayer, our bodies rise up with all the strength of its power, while our hearts and voices swell to proclaim the greatness of the Lord to all in heaven and on earth. We stand because God's promise to be with us stands, and we stand in witness to that promise.

We are made to rejoice in our God and our God in us. Magnificat!

Jesus, joy of the poor of spirit, raise us to new life.

Reflection

1. "Mary is in love." How do I know this? What does it mean?

2. How did abandonment make Mary confident? How does abandonment make us free?

3. Can I stand in the presence of God and pray the *Magnificat?* Can I experience God rejoicing in me? Can I experience my rejoicing in God?

June 14

FLAG DAY

As a grade-school child, I learned that the Church is one, holy, catholic, and apostolic. The sense that these words conveyed to me as a youngster was that all people were welcome in our Church, not just certain people.

The street on which I grew up was a street of immigrants. The five homes nearest ours had people who were born in Germany, Russia, Canada, Ireland, Italy, Lithuania, Poland, and the United States. I attended Catholic schools that reflected all these nationalities as well as others—Central Americans, South Americans, Afro-Americans, etc. God and the Church were not limited to being "born in America."

I am grateful to all those faithful people of God who taught me the all-encompassing, universal face of God. And I am concerned that children growing up today are getting mixed messages about God and country. In particular, I refer to the flag of our country. To freely display the flag in private homes, businesses, or public places is the prerogative of those who own those places. Where the flag is not appropriate and where it is giving a mixed message is in the sanctuaries of our Catholic churches. The flag of the United States and the flag of the Vatican are prominent civil symbols that reflect national ties and allegiances. They are both in the sanctuaries of many Catholic churches.

The church is the place for all people to worship the God of all. Every symbol used in the church building should reflect the universal nature of the Church as the people of God. The church is the place where the Eucharist is offered, a place where we express our participation in the act of redemption that Jesus Christ made for every member of the human race.

In 1978 the bishops of the United States reminded us of this call to be one Church throughout the world and called for the removal of national symbols (flags) from our churches:

> Although the art and decoration of the liturgical space will be that of the local culture, identifying symbols of particular cultures, groups or nations are not appropriate as permanent parts of the liturgical environment. While such symbols might be used for a particular occasion or holiday, they should not regularly constitute a part of the environment of common prayer.[13]

The United States is almost unique in displaying the national flag within its churches. Few other countries in the world do this in their Catholic churches. Even St. Peter's Basilica in Rome does not have the Vatican flag in the sanctuary. Our churches are places of worship, not political arenas. We gather in our churches to pray for all people and to give expression to our belief in God's love for all. In our churches Christ is present sacramentally in the Eucharist. We genuflect to this presence when entering and leaving church. Every symbol and artwork in the church should reflect this presence. A national flag obscures the universal nature of God and of his Church. The main symbol of our faith is the cross of our Lord Jesus Christ. Let us not allow the universal message of this cross to be obscured by a single-focus flag.

Jesus, protector of all people, raise us to new life.

Reflection

1. Do I see any flag as a civil symbol reflective of national allegiances? Do such symbols belong in a Church reflective of universal love?

2. Is there a flag in my parish church? Is there a cross in my home?

3. Is my parish community receptive to all races and nationalities? How is that expressed? What can I do to encourage this acceptance?

GRADUATIONS:
STANDARDS OF COMMITMENT

June is the month of graduations from kindergarten through graduate school. June 1992 was also the month when the United States Department of Education released the report that an alarming number of American children cannot and do not read, a fact that has not changed since then. We can find the causes for this reading deficiency in many facets of our society, but a key factor is that children aren't encouraged to read. They will read if they are read to, if they see parents reading, if they are brought to the library as often as to the video store, if television is not the center of their family life.

Reading is not the most important thing in our children's lives. The question comes to mind about possible reports that are not made by the United States governmental studies, reports that could only be done in Catholic schools and parishes. Can our Catholic children pray? Do they pray? Can our Catholic children make moral choices? Do they make them?

Our children will pray if we pray with them, if they see us praying, if they are raised in a home where God is mentioned more than sports or MTV or money. If response to God is a once-a-week experience or less for the adults in a home, then children will see God in that limited way and no other. If response to God is a vital, intimate part of the adults' life, then God will be real for the children. No amount of Catholic education can substitute for faith seen alive in the people who are most important to the child.

A mother remarked that her daughter had made her First Communion but did not really understand everything. The girl was bright and well instructed, but nonetheless the body and blood of Christ in the Eucharist is a mystery. The child cannot understand the mystery any more than any of us can. The crucial issue is whether the parents love and appreciate the Eucharist. The child will grow in faith in an atmosphere of faith. Understanding the Eucharist only *begins* with the experience of First Communion.

In a home where faith in the Eucharist is lived, the children will grow in understanding of the real presence of Christ in the form of bread and wine. In a home where prayer is part of daily life, the children will learn to pray. And in a home where faith gets expressed in actions, the children will learn to express their faith by their actions. They will learn that the test of our faith is not in rote answers to theological questions but in the choices we make every day.

Faith lived in daily life becomes the basis for all moral decisions. Following rules will never make us holy, but following Christ will. Our children are faced with serious moral dilemmas very early in life. If we love them and care for their happiness and future, we will teach them how to make good choices. We can't merely hand down sets of rules, of dos and don'ts. We must help them form clear consciences and assist them in measuring all their actions according to the standards of Christ-like love. We must teach them to make choices based upon what we think Christ would do in each situation. We can only teach what we first have learned.

If we wish to take the time to make out our report card as a community this June to measure our progress in passing on the faith to our children, we must honestly look to see if we live our faith each day. If we want our children to pray, then we must start to pray with them. If we want our children to live according to high moral standards, then we must teach them the message of Christ and let them see our personal relationship with him. We must let them see us making hard choices out of love for the person of Jesus and respect for his brothers and sisters.

At this time of school graduations, it is good to keep things in perspective. It is a time to celebrate accomplishments, but our priorities must be clear. The only graduation that ultimately matters is the one from the community of Christic love. That graduation comes when we meet God face to face. Until that time we are in preparation, young and old together. Until that time we study and practice the ways of Jesus so that we can become like Jesus.

Jesus, heart of Christian communities, raise us to new life.

Reflection

1. Even if I am not a parent, for which children am I responsible? What is my commitment in my parish to the faith education of the children?

2. Is God vital in my life? How do I witness to the primacy of God in my daily life?

3. Do I pray? Have I taught someone else to pray? Do I pray with others?

WEDDINGS: UNION OF
BODY AND SPIRIT

The other day I made a phone call to order something. In the course of the conversation, I had to give my name and address. When the person at the other end realized that she was talking to a Sister, she told me a story. For over six months her family had been struggling unsuccessfully with a debilitating illness in the family. One day a friend said to her, "Try praying." She took the advice. Daily Mass became part of her life. What this woman revealed to me was the fact that the Eucharist had changed everything. She said that she could not imagine a day without this prayer again.

The same day that I made this call I read a new sociological study of marriage in the book *Faithful Attraction,* written by a Catholic priest-sociologist, Fr. Andrew Greeley. Among many interesting facts about marriage today, the author gives statistical proof of the effect of prayer between couples. It is amazing. Seventy-five percent of couples who pray together say their marriage is happy, compared to 57 percent of non-prayers who have a happy marriage. "Whether they pray together or not is a very powerful correlate of marital happiness, the most powerful we have yet discovered," Father Greeley concludes. A warm and intense relationship with God encourages a warm and intense relationship with a spouse. Father Greeley also shows that "the highest level of Reconciliation (for those who hit trouble within their marriage) is to be found among those who engage often in joint prayer."[14]

With both the phone call and the book reacting within me, I wondered why we don't use what works. We see the effort and money that go into marriage preparations—gowns, flowers, bands, banquets, and guest lists—and yet none of those concerns affect in the slightest way the future happiness of the marriage.

The spiritual life of the couple is more important and requires more attention than the actual preparation for the wedding. Many couples simply squeeze in the required visits to the priest, considering them a formality like getting their marriage license. Engaged Encounter and other pre-marriage programs are more valuable than a bridal register or a photographer. Married couples know this. Counselors know this. Why do so few engaged couples know this? Are we too hesitant to share the simple facts of what is most meaningful in life and what has helped us most?

I think of that woman on the phone who had a friend who urged her to pray. We seem willing to try anything that might help us except to pray every day. Many of us pray only when there is a crisis. Prayer is not a magic formula that we pull out when we need it to produce the effects we want. If we try praying with such expectations, we will definitely be disappointed. Prayer is friendship with God, and the first fruit it bears is simply the fruit of relationship. Relationship with such a wonderful friend changes and enhances all other relationships in our life.

Prayer with a spouse is in itself a gift of mutual vulnerability. It is a concrete expression of the willingness of two to be one. Nakedness within marriage expresses trust and desire and surrender. Physical nakedness within marriage is a living out of the sacrament of marriage when it is a promise of spiritual and emotional nakedness as well.

Prayer within marriage expresses trust and desire and surrender. In joint prayer the married couple share with each other the deep intricacies of their relationship with Christ. To share prayer with each other is to gift each other with the presence of Christ. Prayer is not an obligation to be fulfilled but an act of faith to be taken. For the couple who pray together, the time of prayer becomes an occasion for passionate intimacy. A marriage lived within the context of prayer becomes a holy union that is a blessing for all peoples.

Jesus, bond of fidelity, raise us to new life.

Reflection

1. If I am married, do I pray with my spouse? Why or why not? What can I do to begin praying?

2. When persons I know are preparing for marriage, how do I contribute to their spiritual preparation? What kind of a wedding would Christ plan?

3. What do the gifts I give for weddings say about the importance of God in a couple's life? How bound am I by the customs and expectations of society? How free am I to encourage the essential rather than the superficial?

MARY, MYSTICAL ROSE

"you open always petal by petal myself as Spring opens
(touching skilfully, mysteriously) her first rose."[15]

June is the month of roses. Of all the flowers of creation,
the rose seems to be the one most expressive of love and
beauty. Poets, artists, composers, and writers of every age
and every culture acclaim the mysterious power of the rose.
In our time a dozen roses is not an everyday gift—it is special and is reserved for those who have touched us with beauty.

The rose is alive with motion and mystery, not permanent and static. As it opens it reveals its depths, displaying
its color and texture. There is no way of knowing, when it
is only a bud tightly closed in on itself, how the rose will be
in its fullness. Even when many roses grow on a single bush,
there is a uniqueness in each flower.

From the earliest recorded traditions in our Church there
has always been a connection between Mary and roses. At
Guadalupe, the sign Mary gave the bishop was an armful of
Castilian red roses. At Fatima, Mary appeared over a wild
rose bush, and at Lourdes, Mary had a yellow rose on each
foot. The word *rosary* means "rose garden." The Litany of
Loreto calls Mary the "Mystical Rose," a title that has been
popular for almost fifteen centuries. Numerous paintings and
sculptures of Mary have roses in them.

It is not surprising that the rose, as an object of great
beauty and mystery, is used for Mary. Mary is a woman
wrapped in beauty and mystery, a woman of passionate love.

The symbolism of the rose is appropriate for her. Mary opened herself to God all her life as a rose opens itself to the sun. The control of the opening is not within the power of the rose; it depends upon the sun. Mary freely surrendered her control and allowed God to open her petal by petal for his use and glory and majesty. No rose could compete with the fullness of the revealed beauty of Mary.

It is not coincidence that we put "mystic" and "rose" together when referring to Mary. A mystic is one who has direct experience of God. It was that relationship which gave Mary her openness to mystery and her share in the beauty of God. Like all the accolades of Mary, "Mystical Rose" is both a title for Mary and the reminder of a call for us. All the roses in the world are as nothing compared to the beauty to which we have been called. If we thought of ourselves as flowers at all, most of us would hardly put ourselves in the rose category. We feel more like dandelions or wild flowers. However, in the eyes of God we are immeasurably more precious than the rarest variety of rose—infinitely so, since by grace we share in the beauty of God.

Again, if we were asked if we are mystics, most of us would look puzzled that the question is even being raised. We're not the type. Yet, as Christians, we are all called to live in the direct experience of God; our sharing in his divine life is the foundation of our mysticism. So we should be comfortable thinking of ourselves as mystics as well as roses.

As mystics, we simply abide in the presence of God, knowing that we are loved and cared for and cherished beyond our capacity to imagine. As brothers and sisters of one another, we abide in the presence of God, knowing that every other person is also loved and cared for and cherished beyond our capacity to imagine. To accept the call of mysticism is to accept the call of unlimited love for one another. Mysticism involves a deep relationship with God and with all the children of God. It is responsibility as well as relationship.

Mysticism isn't a reality that happens to some people and not to others. Nothing "just happens" in the plan of God.

Every experience of grace, which is the life of God within us, is a free gift from God. No amount of human effort or good will or generous actions deserves grace; it is always infinitely beyond our capabilities. Mysticism is grace, it is being with God in a very special way. It also is gift and cannot be earned.

However, we can prepare ourselves for the possibility of grace. We can have our light ready and our table set for the coming of our Lord and lover. We prepare by being faithful disciples of our Lord Jesus. This means that we study his words, pray with him, and try to live in a way that is consistent with his gospel message of truth and love for all people. We prepare for the moments of mystical experience by fidelity to the ordinary daily acts of showing love to others and giving worship to God.

To understand mysticism, it helps to look at some of the people who have preceded us in this experience, the men and women whom history has recognized as mystics. We can reflect on the reality of mysticism in their lives. The great saints who had extraordinary mystical experiences did not base their faith on those moments. In fact, some, like St. Teresa of Avila, begged God to take away the extraordinary experiences. She understood that relationship with God does not rest on the unusual. Mysticism does not remove us from the human experience; it simply brings all of the human into the divine.

We have a God who became incarnate in Jesus Christ. We have a God who valued the human so much that Jesus became one with it. The human is important to God. We experience God as mystics when we experience our humanity in its fullness being touched by the divine.

To live as mystics means that we wake each day with grateful hearts and kneel to acknowledge the One to whom we are grateful. We pray to God in simple human words, in wordless yearning, or in silent surrender. We read the word of God, allow it to penetrate our hearts, and attempt to live it in health and in sickness, in light and in darkness. In the evening we again kneel with grateful hearts to acknowledge the One to whom we are grateful. This is the daily rhythm of mysticism.

When we live our days this way, there will be times when our God will unexpectedly break through the ordinary and touch us in a way more real than the physical touch of another person. We will recognize our God, we will feel the touch, and we will know God and be known by God.

Mystical Rose, pray for us.

Jesus, arouser of mystics, raise us to new life.

Reflection

1. Has God opened me "petal by petal"? Have I surrendered to such vulnerability?

2. What was my last mystical experience with God, that is, when was the last time I knew that God was present to me? What did I feel at the time? What do I feel now?

3. Do I kneel and thank God at the beginning and end of each day? Are these moments important to me? to God? If I don't kneel each day, would I like to begin? Will I?

JULY TO SEPTEMBER: INTRODUCTION

Jesus, Lamb of God, have mercy on us.

July

The incarnation of God in Jesus and the death and resurrection of Jesus conquered sin but did not remove sin from the world. We still have our free wills, which can and do choose the way of evil over the way of good. The act of redemption is completed, but our constant need for mercy is part of everyday life. As we need to breathe in order to live, so we need to cry for mercy to live as Christians.

The cry for mercy comes from individuals and from communities of believers. For some people throughout the world, July 1 begins a forty-day fast asking for the conversion of the Church to the nonviolent ways of Christ. We are not helpless in the face of violence; we can meet it with nonviolent resistance. *Jesus, victim of violence, have mercy on us.*

Every victim of violence calls forth compassion from us, but none more than a child. St. Maria Goretti, resisting a rapist, was brutally attacked and murdered at the age of twelve. Many of our children suffer in the same way. Abuse of children demands a response from us. We give the same one Jesus gave—we love back. *Jesus, lover of enemies, have mercy on us.*

The murder of one child is a tragedy beyond comprehension. The mass murder of thousands of children through nuclear war is a tragedy beyond comprehension. In our lifetime we have witnessed both. On July 16, 1945, the nuclear age began with the testing of the first atomic bomb in the New Mexico desert. But even this evil does not leave us without hope. On July 16, 1251, Mary appeared to St. Simon Stock, promising her prayers for grace and protection. And so we gather on this day under the patronage of Our Lady of Mount Carmel to pray for protection from any future use of atomic weapons and for forgiveness for their past use. *Jesus, conqueror of evil, have mercy on us.*

In this world's darkness, disciples of Jesus Christ can be light for others. Mary of Magdala was a faithful disciple, one who received the light of Christ and spread the light of Christ. She followed Jesus even to the cross and became the first witness to his resurrection. But rather than let her bask in the delight of his presence, Jesus sent her out immediately to tell the others. The call to discipleship is a call to mission, which is our call as Christians. *Jesus, strength of disciples, have mercy on us.*

August

One of the most treacherous characteristics of evil is its ability to disguise itself. We do evil and fail to see it as evil. We dropped an atomic bomb on Hiroshima on August 6, 1945, and celebrated it! To this day our failure to acknowledge our use of atomic bombs on Japan as an immoral use of force poisons our consciences. Until we repent of this sin, we will not be free from the fear of repeating it. *Jesus, redeemer of the sins of the world, have mercy on us.*

On August 9, 1945, we dropped a second atomic bomb on Nagasaki, Japan. The large Christian community there responded with hope and forgiveness, accepting their share in the sacrifice of the Lamb of God. One man in particular, Dr. Takashi Nagai, spoke eloquently by his words and by his life of the redemptive value of suffering. Others found hope in his hope. A people survived. A devastated community was reborn. *Jesus, hope of the faithful, have mercy on us.*

Within a week of the anniversary of these atomic bombings, we celebrate another cosmic reality—the assumption of Mary's body into heaven. The contrast is obvious: God's glorification of life matches our destruction of life. God is God. God will not allow Mary's body to corrupt. Destruction will not have the final word. The work of God's hands will give God glory and praise. Through a woman it is accomplished. In this woman we see our possibility and our future. *Jesus, restorer of humanity, have mercy on us.*

Even before we see God face to face in eternity as Mary does, we can experience daily the fullness of redemption in the Eucharist. At every Mass we are present at the sacrifice of Calvary. We are there as Jesus offers himself to the Father for our sake. This is the incarnation of mercy. We receive mercy at its greatest moment in history. *Jesus, manna from heaven, have mercy on us.*

September

This is the month when schools begin another year. For many it is a return to familiar grounds, but not for all. For some little ones it will be their first time in a classroom. For adolescents it may be their first day in high school; for many young adults entering college, it is their first time away from home. Do they have something real to fear from the educational system itself? Not all children grow in the educational process. Too many fall through the cracks and harden into children experienced with failure. They move from year to year in a pattern of competition that leaves them feeling unaccepted and unloved. This is not the way Christ treated children. It is not the way he showed us. *Jesus, lover of children, have mercy on us.*

When we have failed our children or one another, we need to repent in sorrow, not guilt. The Feast of Our Lady of Sorrows brings us into the presence of Mary with this attitude of responsibility for past sins and with hope for the conversion of all. *Jesus, man of sorrows, have mercy on us.*

Defensiveness about our possessions has led us to arms and wars and conflicts. One way to give up this defensiveness is to give up our possessions. Voluntary poverty is a hallmark of any serious peacemaker. The connection is vital. The work of peace is based on trust in God. Trust in God's material providence leads to trust in God's spiritual providence. *Jesus, provider of all good things, have mercy on us.*

Violence on an international scale is reflected in our arms build-up. Violence on a personal scale is reflected in our loss of consciousness about the holiness of sexuality. This shows in our patterns of sexual behavior and vocabulary. Focus on reverence for the human body has been replaced by focus on invasion and conquest. Sex has become a sport and is spoken of as if it were a sport. But to make sex a sport is to make it a violent sport. We were created for more than sport; we were created for love and will be fulfilled in love. Our lives are meant to be stories of love. *Jesus, intimate friend, have mercy on us.*

July 1

FORTY-DAY FAST FOR
CHRISTIAN NONVIOLENCE

For many Christians throughout the world, July 1 is the beginning of a forty-day fast for recognition of the truth of Christian nonviolence.[16] Since it was begun in 1983, the fast has spread throughout many Churches and countries. The purpose of the fast is to beg God that the universal Church will declare in ecumenical council that violence is not the way of Jesus Christ. The fast is really a cry for the truth of Christ's message to be proclaimed.

The forty-day fast ends on August 9, a day of great significance in the Christian Church. On August 9, 1942, Edith Stein, a Carmelite sister called Sister Teresia Benedicta of the Cross, was killed in the gas chambers at Auschwitz by Christians. On August 9, 1943, Franz Jaegerstaetter, a Catholic father of two small children was beheaded in Berlin by Christians for refusing to serve in Hitler's army. On August 9, 1945, Nagasaki, the oldest and largest Christian community in Japan, was chosen as a target for the atomic bomb and devastated by Christians. The plane was piloted by a Catholic.

There have been many other dates of shame in the history of Christianity, but this date of August 9 is too important to pass without notice. It is too tragic to pass without repentance. It is too frightening to ever be repeated.

How will fasting change what has already happened? Fasting, like any other form of penance, is ultimately an expression of love; it is not punishment for evil that has been done. Evil does not end with the end of an evil act. Its ripple effect can travel from generation to generation until something breaks the cycle. Fasting is an attempt to break the cycle.

When we fast we are saying that we want to focus ourselves in a specific way on God. In a very real way God will be more important to us than food or drink. When we feel hungry, we turn our minds and hearts to God. If the whole fast becomes an obsession with hunger, it is better not to fast.

The way of fasting is a way of prayer. We freely give up for a time the physical life-support of food as a reminder of the One who is the source and support of all life. Daily prayer is the backbone of the fast. Without it we become paralyzed.

The specific way of fasting—liquid diet, one meal per day, no meat, one day on bread and water, no cigarettes, no movies, no alcohol, etc.—can be different for each individual. Age, health, and daily schedule all affect our choices in fasting. Anyone who fasts or undertakes any form of physical penance ought to have a spiritual director. The greater blessing is in obedience, not in mortification or endurance.

It is a risk to fast, not for reasons of health, but because during this time of fasting in our bodies, we begin to look at what it means to fast from violence in our spirits. Fasting is a risk because of the responsibility we must carry once we understand the nonviolent way of Jesus. Knowledge carries responsibility for fidelity. It is a risk to fast because we must face the possibility of our own conversion.

To open ourselves to the possibility of being changed is the most heroic adventure we can undertake. Conversion implies a leap into vulnerability; it faces us with the challenge of freedom from society's standards; it invites us to seek union with God in passionate love.

If forty days of fasting seems extreme, we need to measure them against the extreme of Jesus Christ's love for us expressed in his passion and death. In the old Church calendar, July 1 used to be the Feast of the Precious Blood of Jesus. This feast reminds us that while we may shed a few pounds during the fast, Jesus Christ, who was sinless, shed his blood to the last drop for us.

For centuries Christians have denied the implications of this way of nonviolent love and have chosen to take others' blood in violence rather than to follow their Lord and shed their own blood in love. This fast is undertaken in order that individually we may be converted to the nonviolent ways of Jesus, and that communally we may accept and teach his nonviolent way.

Jesus, victim of violence, have mercy on us.

Reflection

1. What is the purpose of fasting? What does it express? What does it effect?

2. Do I resist change and conversion? Why? What can I do to open myself to the possibility of conversion?

3. Am I interested in finding out more about this forty-day fast? Am I willing to participate? Do I see the value of a Church commitment to nonviolence?

July 6

ST. MARIA GORETTI

In 1904 in Corinaldi, Italy, a twelve-year-old girl from a poor family resisted an attempted rape until she was stabbed to death. Her canonization as St. Maria Goretti made her story known universally. The official meaning of the rite of canonization is that the Church believes that the person raised to the level of saint is with God.

There can be no doubt that an innocent child brutally murdered is with God. The doubt that does arise is usually doubt in God. Where was God when Maria was being attacked? Where was God in those moments of unspeakable fear and pain? Where was God when the wounds from the stabbing could not be closed and healed? Where was God when Maria's mother cradled the dead body of her daughter in her arms for the last time?

Where is God today when one out of every three girls under the age of eighteen in the United States is abused, when one out of every five boys is abused? Where is God when children are tormented and tortured in their own homes? Where is God when children are not even safe within their churches?

God is with us always. We are taught that as children. If we believe it, then we believe God was with Maria Goretti when she was attacked and God is with every other child who suffers abuse. In Jesus, God is not only with the children but suffers with them, weeps with them, and holds them in his arms even when it appears that the only arms around them are those of hatred and cruelty.

We must believe in spite of all our feelings of hopelessness and despair that no one and no thing can take us from the hand of God except our own free will to sin. There is no sin of any kind on the part of a child in a situation of abuse.

This last statement must seem obvious, but it must be said clearly and loudly. The insidious nature of abuse is such that the children think it is their fault that they are getting raped or fondled, beaten or neglected.

As an adult, the perpetrator has power over the child, extending even to power over the child's mind. In physical abuse the child is told, "You deserve this." "It's your own fault you are getting beaten." "It's your fault there is a divorce." "You are bad and evil." "If you would act differently this wouldn't be happening." The reasons are endless. The child will get beaten if it rains, if the mail is late, if the husband comes home drunk, if the husband comes home sober. There is always an excuse.

When the abuse is sexual, the child is fed different lies. "You really like this. You enjoy this. If you tell others, they will blame you. This is how we show that we love each other." Like Maria Goretti, most children will resist an attack, at least the first time, if they are old enough. Often the threat of punishment suppresses their resistance. In some cases the abuse begins early in life, so the child knows nothing else.

This evil process comes back to haunt abused children as they grow into adulthood, and they see what they had to do to survive as cooperation with the evil. They blame themselves. This is not right. They were in no way responsible, no matter what they did or what was done to them. As children they were victims.

It is necessary in our day to break through the shame that is associated with the sexual abuse of children. Being forced to live with this shame creates guilt in the children who suffer it. Loss of self-esteem and lack of self-acceptance keep them emotionally victimized long after the assault. They need to know that it is not their fault they were abused, even if the perpetrator is a member of their own family. They were not loved and protected as they should have been. We must make sure that every potential victim of this terrible experience knows that abuse is an adult crime and children are its victims.

Nurturance and security are as important to life as bread and water. Abused children are denied these basic rights, and so their sense of self-esteem is dangerously low. We learn who we are in relationship to others. Abused children have been denied healthy relationships, and so they are confused as to who they are. In acts of abuse, both sexual and physical, the boundaries of children's bodies are violated. In the process the boundaries of their spirits are also violated, and so they sometimes go through life less able to perceive or respect the boundaries of others. These children do not have the experience of being loved and accepted for who they are; they only have the experience of being used for the pleasure of others.

Maria Goretti did not suffer in this way. She did not have a history of abuse. It would seem that she grew up in a loving family with strong religious values. This may explain why Maria resisted being raped. Although she was physically weaker than her assailant, she was morally stronger. She had a sense of self and of God that helped her resist.

Most children who are abused suffer over and over until their sense of self is ravaged as much as their bodies. Through the intercession of St. Maria Goretti we pray that we will put a stop to this evil in our society and protect our children. This means that we must inform ourselves about abuse until we are able to recognize its signs. It means that we must accept responsibility for reporting abuse of any kind. We pray, as Jesus taught us, for our enemies, so we pray for the perpetrators of child abuse. We hold them responsible for their actions, but we do not judge. Even here we pray to forgive.

We pray also for the parents of children who have been abused or even killed in the act of abuse. To give comfort seems beyond our human ability, no matter the empathy we feel. May Christ in infinite love and gracious tenderness hold them and their wounded children in the palm of his hand and may the Spirit of God heal them.

Jesus, lover of enemies, have mercy on us.

Reflection

1. When the innocent suffer, what is my reaction? Do I blame God? Do I blame others? Do I feel helpless? Do I allow this feeling to paralyze me?

2. Do I know enough about child abuse to recognize the signs? What can I do to become better informed?

3. Do I take responsibility for the protection of children in my sphere of influence? Do I guarantee their safety? When I see abuse, do I report it? Do I pray for offenders as well as victims?

TRINITY TEST AND
MOUNT CARMEL

On July 16, 1945, the first atomic bomb, blasphemously named "Trinity," was detonated at 5:29:45 Mountain War Time in the New Mexico desert, about eighty miles southeast of Albuquerque. The bomb cost $56 million, and over six thousand people were involved in its production. The nineteen-kiloton explosion ushered the world into the atomic age. All life on earth has been touched by the event that took place there.

Reflecting on the atomic blast years later, J. Robert Oppenheimer, the genius behind the bomb, uttered the words from the Bhagavad Gita: "Now I am become death, the shatterer of worlds."[17] We don't know fully what this man thought after he created the bomb, but we do know that he, along with many of the scientists who worked on the creation of the atomic bombs that were dropped on Hiroshima and Nagasaki, tried to get the government to demonstrate the potential destructiveness of the bombs to the Japanese rather than use them on their civilian populations. Later he opposed the development of the hydrogen bomb and worked ceaselessly against the production of any other weapon of mass destruction.

In 1947, in a lecture at the Massachusetts Institute of Technology, Oppenheimer said: "The physicists have known sin and this is a knowledge which they cannot lose." In 1967, when questioned about the Nuclear Test Ban Treaty, he replied: "It's twenty years too late. We should have signed it the day after Trinity." Many scientists, including Einstein, felt it should never have been invented. Those scientists who worked on it seemed to have been seduced by the technological challenge of creating the bomb without dwelling on the consequences of using it on live human beings.

The scientists weren't sure at the time of the explosion if the test would be safe for the citizens of New Mexico. General Leslie Groves of the United States Army had made a deal with the governor of New Mexico to evacuate the state if necessary. Citizens of New Mexico knew nothing about this plan or the test until the residents of the surrounding towns felt the blast and saw the light. A blind girl in the area saw light for the first and only time in her life. Ranchers immediately saw the effect of the radiation in their livestock.

Commenting on that first explosion in the desert of New Mexico, Oppenheimer said: "We knew the world would not be the same. A few people laughed. A few people cried. Most people were silent."

The time has come to be silent no longer. The Trinity test is over; the work of peace is not. It is not enough to criticize the past; we are responsible for the present and the future. Every year since 1990 a group of people have gathered at the Trinity site in New Mexico to take responsibility for the past and the future. They come from Hiroshima in Japan, from Ireland, Northern Ireland, Canada, and all parts of the United States. They gather on this day in remembrance of two events: one is the Trinity test, and the other is the apparition of Mary, the Mother of God, to St. Simon Stock on July 16, 1251, which the Church commemorates yearly on the Feast of Our Lady of Mount Carmel. The concurrence of these two events is not coincidence. God has a plan of salvation; there are no coincidences in the plan of God. God knew we would need Mary on this day. We accept God's gift of mercy through Mary.

This day is commemorated in the desert in prayer and hope. What was scarred earth has become holy ground. People from all over the world join in this Mount Carmel prayer in their own cities and countries. Individuals confined to their homes join with all the others in prayers of hope and petition for the protection of our fragile world and for the conversion of all our hearts to the Beatitudes of Jesus. Many parishes keep their churches open for the twenty-four hours of prayer.

The particular forms of prayer recommended for this day are the Eucharist and the rosary. In the Eucharist we offer with Jesus his body and blood to the Father in atonement for sin. With the rosary we keep before us continuously the life, death, and resurrection of Jesus in the presence of his mother.

Because we are not helpless in the face of evil and because we believe that Christ has overcome evil with love, we dare to approach God and one another with hope for forgiveness for the evil of the first atomic bomb and for protection from the potentially bitter fruits of that evil. Even this evil does not leave us without hope. We will not be silent; our voices are raised in prayer and in witness.

Jesus, conquerer of evil, have mercy on us.

Reflection

1. Am I willing to face the facts of the danger of nuclear testing and production? What can I do in response to these facts?

2. Are there times when I sin by silence? Am I comfortable in my silence? Am I responsible for my failure to speak out?

3. Am I responsible for praying for world peace? On July 16, can I pray the rosary and participate in the Eucharist? Can I ask others to join me?

July 22

MARY MAGDALEN

Christ's love is given to us in abundance, beyond all our expectations and merits. We cannot earn it or even deserve it. We receive love and by God's grace we respond. Then the miraculous happens, and our very response, which is a gift in the first place, becomes an occasion for increased response from Christ. The constant interplay between our response and Christ's response is the passion of love, human and divine.

Mary Magdalen is the Gospel woman we usually associate with such passion. The factual information about her is slight, but it is sufficient to let us understand her place in the life of Christ. Biblical scholars generally agree that she was most probably not the woman of Luke 7:36-50, who washed the feet of Jesus and who was a public sinner, the one who loved much because she was forgiven much. History romantically and mistakenly associates this repentant woman with Mary Magdalen.

We do know that Jesus cast seven demons out of Mary. What that actually means is not specifically recorded. It could refer to possession by the devil or physical or mental illness; it does not necessarily mean sin. It is clear that Jesus freed Mary from a severe malady.

We know that Mary Magdalen was at the foot of the cross with Mary, the mother of Jesus. From the rest of the Gospel narrative we know that at this time in Jerusalem it was not safe for the disciples of Jesus to publicly acknowledge their relationship with him. It was a time of terror and fear for the Christians there.

Mary Magdalen stayed at the cross because Jesus was there and for no other reason. There could not have been another reason strong enough. Mary loved Jesus and she believed in him; she couldn't leave him, even though most of his special Twelve had betrayed, denied, or abandoned him. It is not stretching the imagination or the Gospel story to presume the confusion, anxiety, and pain that Mary was experiencing. At the very least it took tremendous courage for her to risk the jeers and threats of the executioners, the other soldiers, and the crowd to stay with Jesus to the end. It also took faith to believe in Jesus when there was no external evidence to support such faith.

We sometimes confuse faith with understanding and with feeling secure and confident in certain beliefs or about certain persons. Mary may or may not have felt this way beneath the cross. The relevant fact is that she stayed. That is faith—not to feel good or to know clearly, but to be there, to stay with Christ no matter what happens. Mary, by her presence at the foot of the cross, shows us that Christianity is not a "feel good" religion but a commitment of enduring love.

The next mention we have of Mary is at the sepulcher. When Joseph of Arimathea places the body of Jesus in the tomb and rolls the large stone across the entrance, Mary Magdalen is there with the other Mary. Even in death Mary will not leave the body of her Beloved. There are times in our lives when all we can do is sit in the presence of one another and of our God. We cannot change or fix an experience of pain, but we can be at peace in the midst of it and be in the presence of our God in silence.

Finally we know that Mary is a witness to the resurrection. After the Sabbath, Mary is back at the tomb with her spices to anoint the body of Jesus. The tomb is guarded.

Armed soldiers can be intimidating and threatening, especially to women. Not this time—the guards are as dead men with shock and fright, the stone is rolled back, the tomb is empty, and angels are standing by. The women are sent back to tell the disciples that Jesus is risen and will meet them in Galilee.

Mary stays, venturing into the tomb to see for herself. She is disconsolate, thinking that someone has stolen the body of her Lord. Weeping, she tells the angels that her Lord has been taken and she doesn't know where to find him. Love that has endured witnessing the brutal crucifixion is now desperate. Mary cannot live without her Lord. She has made the drastic shift from following Christ to being unable to live or breathe without him. Here is the heart of discipleship: Mary will search until she finds her Lord.

Mary will not stay weeping. She will find Jesus; she will search and she will ask everyone where he can be found. She starts with the gardener, "Sir, if you have carried him away, tell me where you have laid him, and I will take him away" (John 20:15). With a single word the resurrected Jesus reveals himself—"Mary!"

"Ask, and it will be given you; search, and you will find; knock, and the door will be opened for you" (Luke 11:9). Did Jesus plan from all eternity that Mary would be the first to witness his resurrection? Or did Jesus simply respond to the one who seemed to be searching the hardest to find him? Could the heart of Jesus be indifferent to the heart of one who stayed with him and with his mother under the cross when they needed support the most? The Gospel is showing us how Jesus responds to those who seek him and who believe in him when times are hard and society is rejecting his way.

The Gospel shows us the way Jesus responds: with the gift of personal, intimate union. Jesus calls Mary by her name; he says her name in such a way that she knows it is her Lord. We need to listen to the way Jesus says our name so that we will recognize it and also recognize him when he says it.

Mary and Jesus knew each other and loved each other, and only a word was necessary to restore all the hope that the darkness of the crucifixion had tried to destroy. Life is restored and renewed and redeemed. Union with Christ is the bond that holds life together when the darkness seems overpowering.

Following upon this moment of revelation and joyful reunion, both Jesus and Mary turn immediately to mission. Always the mission of spreading the word of God takes precedence over anything else. Mary is sent out to the others with a message, "Say to them that I am ascending to my Father and your Father, to my God and your God" (John 20:17). Jesus Christ, the Son of God and Word of God made flesh, is sharing God with us; his Father is our Father and his God is our God. Like Mary Magdalen, we must witness to the One we have seen with our own eyes and known with our own hearts.

Jesus, strength of disciples, have mercy on us.

Reflection

1. What does it mean "to believe in Jesus when there is no external evidence to support such faith"? Do I have this faith in Jesus? How do I know I have it?

2. Do I expect Christianity to be a "feel good" religion? Do I complain and lose heart when endurance and commitment are required?

3. What name does Jesus call me? What name do I call him? To whom does he send me?

August 6

HIROSHIMA

On August 6, 1945, the first atomic bomb was exploded over Hiroshima, Japan. The conscience of the world has been poisoned to this day by our failure to see this use of force as immoral. The clouds of that bomb have never dissipated. We still live in fear of it. The reason is that we have not allowed ourselves to be set free from the threat of using it again. We will not be set free from our fear until we repent of the evil of using the bomb again.

Repentance, or turning away from evil, is crucial to freedom. When Jesus began his public ministry with the word "Repent," he was not trying to lay burdens on us. He loved us too much to do that. Jesus came urging repentance because he wanted to help us get the heaviness of hatred off our backs and the poison of fear out of our hearts.

We need the heaviness of the atomic bombs off our backs. Those scientists who touched the bombs with their hands knew their evil. The atomic bombs were dropped on Japan against the express desire of over two-thirds of the scientists who developed them. The pilots and servicemen on the plane that dropped the first atomic bomb on Hiroshima returned to base shaken by the devastation, asking that another one not be used. They were not listened to. Nagasaki took the brunt of the next one.

Those Japanese who suffered the effects of the bomb need the burden of its heaviness lifted. A woman who was outside the area of Hiroshima's devastation but who lost family and friends, Sister Kayoko Shibata, said: "Through this experience, I am convinced that true peace comes only through Christ. I am not inclined to only scream, 'No more Hiroshima!' I want to do more than appeal to anti-war feeling, I want to tell everybody that Christ is the only one who can give us true peace, for that is the way to peace I have experienced."[18]

We need to listen to these people who suffered and found Christ with them in their pain. We need to listen to them and learn of the pain that must not be repeated. We need to listen to them and learn the only way to peace—participation in the very mystery of Christ's own suffering love that did not retaliate but endured evil with love.

Revenge destroys both the avenger and the victim. And destruction is not the way of Christ. There is nothing in the New Testament that supports the use of force to protect any thing or anyone. The message of Jesus is that life is infinitely valuable, and only God has the ultimate authority over life at every stage, from conception to death.

As we observe the anniversary of Hiroshima, we need to look into our own hearts. Perhaps we will find the strength to repent individually of the violence in our lives, so that one day we can repent communally of the violence we employ as a nation by our continual recourse to the power of force rather than to the power of love.

Jesus, redeemer of the sins of the world, have mercy on us.

Reflection

1. Do I think nuclear weapons are compatible with the gospel teachings of Jesus? Is it Christian to build a nuclear weapon? to threaten to use one? to actually use one?

2. Is hatred a heavy burden? Does it poison my spirit? Does it cripple my heart?

3. What personal violence is there in my life? Do I repent of it? Do I want to stop it? What can I do to achieve this end?

August 9

NAGASAKI

Nagasaki, like Hiroshima, is usually associated in our minds with the atomic bomb that was dropped on it in August 1945. In Nagasaki the Peace Park, the rebuilt Urakami Cathedral, and other memorials stand in mute testimony to the second atomic bomb. But Nagasaki is far more than a witness to the devastating effects of war. Nagasaki is a witness to the hope of people even in the midst of pain. It is witness to the redemptive value of suffering. Especially for Catholics, Nagasaki is holy ground. It is a place that experienced religious persecution for almost four centuries. The wonder is that it is a place that speaks of courage and joy and hope.

On August 15, 1549, St. Francis Xavier landed in Japan near the present port of Nagasaki. The evangelization of Japan began. Many Japanese were converted. At first Christians were accepted, but as they grew in number, persecution began. Near the end of the sixteenth century political leaders began to fear that the growing influence of Christianity would diminish the power of the emperor. Hundreds of Japanese were martyred. All foreign priests were expelled. Eventually the Christians went underground and became known as the Hidden Christians. For seven generations faithful laity passed on baptism and faith to their children. They lived in prayer and in hope. They believed that God would free them one day.

In 1864, with the opening of Japan's ports to the world, the foreign missionaries returned and found the faith alive and the Christians secretly active and numerous. The Oura Church built at this time still stands. It is in this church that the Hidden Christians, those who had kept the faith in secret for three hundred years, declared themselves to Father Petitjean in 1865. The Christians came out of hiding at this time but met another period of persecution before they were finally granted religious freedom in 1872.

In 1945, Japanese Christians were once again called to suffer. The largest Christian settlement in Japan was destroyed by the bomb of August 9, 1945. Urakami Cathedral, built over a forty-year period by the descendants of the Hidden Christians, was demolished in nine seconds. A city became a nuclear wasteland. A city now needed to be reborn from the ashes.

The man credited by the Japanese as the one largely responsible for the rebuilding of hope among the people of Nagasaki was Dr. Takashi Nagai. While a student at the University Hospital in Nagasaki, Dr. Nagai was attracted to Catholicism through the faith of the Moriyama family, with whom he boarded. He struggled with this new faith before finally surrendering to the God of love and being baptized. A strong influence in his conversion was the daughter of the Moriyamas, Midori, whom Takashi later married.

Midori and Takashi loved each other deeply and had a happy marriage and two children at the time the bomb fell. Takashi referred to his wife as "faithful Midori," and when he was with her he always felt he was in the presence of holiness.

When the bomb exploded over Nagasaki, Dr. Nagai was at the hospital, which was badly hit. With only a few surviving doctors and nurses, he worked day and night in the nightmare of those first days after the bomb. Because of the hundreds of injured and dying victims, it was three days before he got to his own home, which was only a few miles from the hospital. There he found a small pile of charred bones and a melted rosary in what was his kitchen. It was Midori. She had died saying her rosary while working in her kitchen. Holding her ashes, Dr. Nagai cried and thanked Mary for being with his beloved Midori when she died. Their two children were spared because they were in the country with their grandmother.

With other survivors Dr. Nagai began building hope in the nuclear waste. He began building a city. He kept a vision of a loving God and of the value of making the effort to keep on loving. Dr. Nagai said that it was prayer that gave him this vision of the redemptive dimension of suffering and death.

Within a year Dr. Nagai's own health became worse because of the leukemia he had contracted from using an X-ray machine before the bomb fell. He spent his last years in a little hut praying, writing, painting, and receiving visitors, encouraging those in despair to trust in the God of love. Dr. Nagai lived the words of the Buddhist parable "You best meet the Supernatural if you make your heart like a hut that is empty of everything but the bare essentials."[19]

Dr. Nagai helped the people of Nagasaki to witness to the power of redemptive suffering. The witness is still visible in the city today. There is no explaining the hope and joy that emanate from all those places made holy by the suffering of so many.

Resurrection comes not from understanding but from faith in the impossible. Nagasaki has experienced resurrection. We thank God and pray that we also may be faithful when it is our time to witness.

Jesus, hope for the faithful, have mercy on us.

Reflection

1. What is the redemptive value of suffering? What was it for Christ? What is it for me?

2. Do I value and appreciate freedom of religion? Do I work to maintain my freedom of religion from the subtle pressures of society?

3. What can I do to make my heart "like a hut that is empty of everything but the bare essentials"? What step will I take this week to prepare myself for abandonment to the ways of God and the person of Jesus?

August 15

THE ASSUMPTION OF MARY

A few years after the tragedy of World War II left fifty-one million people dead and countless others without countries, homes, families, or hope, the Catholic Church proclaimed the dogma of the Assumption, which declares that Mary, the Mother of God, was assumed into heaven after her time on earth was finished. This dogma recognizes the infinite value God placed on the human body of his mother, and through her on all our bodies. This dogma celebrates the reality of the call of humanity to share in divinity.

Does the timing of the proclamation of this mystery of Mary's assumption and God's desire to share eternity with humanity seem unusual after the massive disregard for humanity that the world experienced during the war? Since the time of Mary's death, the tradition among the faithful has always been that Mary's body was assumed into heaven. Why, after all this time of general belief in the fact of the assumption, did the Church now decide to state the obvious?

The Spirit of God blows when it will, and we ponder the ways of this Spirit to better cooperate with them. Perhaps after all the sin and pain of the war and the years immediately preceding and following it, the universal cry of despair and disregard for the sacredness of the human body were met by God's cry of hope and restoration of the dignity of the human body.

Now we are a generation away from that particular war. We have had other wars in many foreign countries and continue to settle most international conflicts with guns and bombs. Violence is in our streets and in our homes. Injustice and lack of compassion leave many to starve physically and emotionally. Hatred claims its victims daily. Yet we celebrate in these same times the assumption of Mary, body and soul, into heaven. This feast is not a denial of the evil within us but rather a declaration of our potential for holiness. As Christians we live out this holiness by supporting life in all its stages and forms and by working against its destruction by any means. As Christians we are also called to celebrate life in its creation, redemption, and glorification.

God created us, male and female, and put us in charge of all the other beautiful works of creation: the sun and moon and stars, which bring light to our days and sparkle to our nights; the land, which nourishes and sustains us; the seas, which refresh and delight us; the rain and snow, which cleanse us; the flowers and plants, which decorate the earth; the fish that color the waters; the animals that roam the fields; and the birds that fill the skies.

Even this beauty and wonder in creation are as nothing compared with the beauty and wonder of a single person. Each of us was made "a little lower than God" (Psalm 8:5). All the sin and pain of the world cannot take that reality from us. All the sin and pain of the world cannot take from us the experience that one of us was assumed into heaven. Mary was sinless but she was still fully human. Her assumption gives dignity to all humanity.

> The princess is decked in her chamber with gold-woven
> robes; in many-colored robes she is led to the king;
> behind her the virgins, her companions, follow.
> With joy and gladness they are led along
> as they enter the palace of the king (Psalm 45:13-15).

She who was the lowly one of God, she who surrendered totally with the words "Here am I, the servant of the Lord"

(Luke 1:38) is the one who is now brought into heaven in glory. Behind Mary, our Mother and Queen, all of us are also brought to God. We are "the virgins, her companions." All of us are virgins in our relationship with God until we meet God face to face and consummate our union for all eternity. We live our virginity by being open and receptive to God at all times, in all places, and under all circumstances.

Mary lived her virginity more perfectly than any other person ever has. As passionately as she embraced virginity she surrendered to consummation. Her assumption into heaven was the visible expression of her final surrender to God. It was the visible expression of God's desire for Mary and of her response in pure grace and sinlessness. What we celebrate in Mary today we anticipate in our own lives. Like Mary, we are created to be fulfilled, to see God face to face, and to live eternally in our resurrected bodies in the presence of God.

We will pass through death in our mortal flesh, but glory awaits us. After we are purified we will be sinless as Mary was, and all the angels of God and the communion of saints will rejoice at our entrance into heaven.

On the Feast of the Assumption we celebrate what has already been and what will be. We celebrate Mary's assumption, we celebrate all those who have gone before us and who are now experiencing perfect wholeness and happiness. We anticipate our own time of resurrection.[20]

"Creation waits with eager longing for the revealing of the children of God" (Romans 8:19). The glory awaits us.

Jesus, restorer of humanity, have mercy on us.

Reflection

1. Do I value my body as God's masterpiece? Do I use it to proclaim the glory of God? Do I celebrate my humanity? Do I celebrate my divinity?

2. What do television and movies say about the beauty of God's creation of men and women? Am I a victim of television and movies? What can I do about it?

3. Do I long to see God face to face as Mary does? What in my life expresses this longing?

DAILY MASS: DAILY GIFT

Long summer days can slow down the rhythm of our lives, especially if the temperature climbs to the sweltering levels. This can be an opportunity to look at the rhythm of our spiritual lives and the place we make for God. We need to do this. Too often day follows day without our ever making deliberate choices about how we will spend our time and energy.

In particular, this can be the opportunity to look at our schedules and consider the possibility of participating in the Eucharist on a daily basis. It can be the time to gather up church bulletins from the local churches to find out where and when we might attend daily Mass.

Before we dismiss this idea too quickly, it would be good to ask why we don't want to consider the possibility. Why should we not make the drastic change of participating in daily Mass? Something in human nature seems to resist change, even if the change would improve things. This resistance keeps us mired in business as usual when change could bring greater happiness and self-satisfaction.

Like its people, the Church also hesitates to change things. However, God's grace is always at work, and new life does come on a regular basis. For some people, changes in the Church come too fast; for some, too slow. The Second Vatican Council was a milestone of change that we are still trying to put into practice.

Of all the changes made at the Council, the first ones to be implemented were those pertaining to the liturgy. In the twenty-five years since, tremendous efforts have been put into the revitalization of the liturgy. Through the combined cooperation of the laity and the clergy, the gifts and talents of many of the people of God now enhance and enrich the celebration of Mass. Those involved with music ministry, the lectors, the Eucharistic ministers, and all the faithful join with the ordained priest to share in offering the sacrifice of Jesus Christ on Calvary for the redemption of this fragile world.

There is no greater prayer that can be offered; there is no more effective way for us to show our love for God and for one another than by uniting with Christ as he offers himself to the Father for our sake. Mohandas Gandhi, a Hindu ascetic, said that Christ's offering of himself for others was the greatest act of love the world has ever seen.[21] As Catholics, we know that we are present at this offering when we participate in the Eucharist.

The deeper issue is not what we say in our theological discussions about the value of the Mass but what we say by our choices and actions. It is hard to reconcile a strong belief in the actual presence of Jesus Christ in the Eucharist and an attitude of indifference toward sharing in the Eucharist with him. If Mass is a celebration of the greatest act of love the world has ever seen, why are we not wearing down a path to daily Mass?

It is not just our physical presence at Mass that makes the difference. The Mass isn't a magic act, producing its full effect regardless of our response. It is our union with Christ in his surrender to his Father that brings us into the mystery of love. When we participate in this spirit, uniting ourselves with Jesus in his offering, then the Eucharist can be the most practical thing we do in the course of our day. It can do more for our family life and social life than any other efforts we can make. It can do more to quiet disturbances in our youth than any clamping down on them. It can do more to stop the violence in our world than massive efforts at law and order. We can bring to the altar illness, pain, loss, and all the confusion of modern life. We can include them in Christ as he offers himself for the redemption of the world.

At Mass, with the other people of God and with Jesus Christ himself, we offer the daily bread of our own lives. We offer them to be transformed into the body and blood of Christ. We receive them back as the manna of each day. Because of this manna and through its effect on us, we grow more and more in the living presence of Jesus Christ in our homes and workplaces.

Then there will be changes in society, not through magic or the direct intervention of God but through us. There will be changes because we will be changed. We will become sensitive to the ways of God and recognize the ways that are not of God. If we stand beside our brothers and sisters in line to receive the body of Christ, we will stand beside them in life, recognizing them as members of the body of Christ among us.

Daily Mass keeps us aware of the spirit of the cross, of Christ's spirit of sacrificial love for us. And it reminds us of our responsibility to show the same love to all our brothers and sisters. Participation in daily Mass is not an escape from reality; it is an escape from the illusion that society holds up to us as reality. It is our daily encounter with truth that sends us out to serve and minister as Christ in this time and in this place. In our liturgy, the final prayer is a command, ''Go in peace.'' Aware of the love in which we have just shared, we go from our churches thanking Christ and expecting to find him peacefully in all the events and people in the day ahead of us.

Jesus, manna from heaven, have mercy on us.

Reflection

1. Do I go to daily Mass? Why or why not?

2. Why is the Eucharist the greatest act of love the world has ever seen? Do I want to be part of it? Am I part of it?

3. Do I participate in the Eucharist with the desire to offer myself for the transformation of the world? Does my offering make any difference? Does Christ's offering make any difference?

SCHOOL DAYS:
TEACHING CHILDREN

One day when I was in kindergarten, a four-year-old girl was working on a wooden pumpkin puzzle. It was time to go home and she still had the unfinished puzzle in front of her. When the teacher told her to quickly put it together, the child said she didn't know how. The teacher impatiently asked, "Why did you take it apart if you didn't know how to put it back together?" As the teacher rushed around to get the other children ready for dismissal, the little girl asked another child to help her and remarked, "How do you know if you can put something together until you take it apart?"

At this time of the year children are going back to their classrooms for another year of learning—hopefully of learning the fun of taking things apart and figuring out how to put them back together. It is important that we not deny them the right to learn in an environment of acceptance and tolerance.

Today the years spent in school mark the parameters of childhood: children begin school as babies and finish as adults. What goes on in schools is crucial to the moral, emotional, and psychological development of our children. It is the responsibility of all of us, not just of teachers or of parents of school-age children.

Theoretically, we claim that the purpose of education is to allow children to develop to their full potential. We say we try to elicit the best from each child. Yet we seem to be more interested in the accumulation of knowledge than in the development of wisdom. We are more interested in having the completed puzzles neatly stacked at the end of the day than in allowing a little girl the time and help she needs to meet her goal. We seem to be more involved in reaching certain objective standards of achievement than in guiding children to know successes and accomplishments. The practice of academic competitiveness often replaces the pursuit of truth. Even in kindergarten the competition to be like the others begins with putting puzzles together.

Such academic competition is contrary to all the principles of sound educational theory, which advocate individual growth in the learning process. It is the ability of learners to think on their own and to evaluate and create that is the sign of educational success. It is the ability of a child to engage in the search for truth that is the sign of educational progress. The value of each child's intellectual achievement is to be measured in its own right, not against another's achievements.

Maria Montessori, one of the most respected and innovative educators of this century, cautioned us:

> An education that is merely a blind struggle between the strong and the weak can produce only inefficient adults. To avoid this, we must substitute more nourishing conditions in our schools for the unfortunate circumstances to which young students are usually subjected. Sadly, children now receive rewards for triumphing over their schoolmates in competitions and excelling in examinations, which allow them to pass from one year to another of monotonous servitude.[22]

The backbone of current educational systems seems to be the report card and the honor roll, both of which emphasize intellectual competitiveness and are the antithesis of the recommendations of Maria Montessori. The rewarding of those children who achieve the highest scores on tests is a disservice to all children.

For those who are less intellectually gifted, school is almost always an experience of being at the bottom. From the time they are in first grade, they know the difference between the Rainbow Reading Group (those who can read) and the Sunshine Reading Group (those who can't read). School is already difficult enough for a child who struggles with every step without the continual discouragement of watching the bright children get honors all along the way.

It is an equally unfair situation for the brighter children because it puts pressure on them not just to learn but to get better grades than other children. We all know that the one with the highest grades is not necessarily the most intelligent, the most responsible, or the most creative child. And we also know that wisdom is not the same thing as intelligence; they are two distinct talents. The question is, Do our children know this?

Are we teaching in a way that fosters each child's growth in wisdom? Are we teaching in a way that respects each child's ability? Are we teaching in a way that helps children learn tolerance and acceptance of themselves and of their classmates?

The key is to measure the progress of each child against that child's starting point, not to measure the end result against an arbitrary standard of achievement. We need to celebrate the achievements of all our children—all their achievements, not just academic ones. Too many children feel that they can never measure up academically to what is expected of them. They feel like Sisyphus pushing that slippery rock up the hill day after day.

The great challenge of education is to find a spark of curiosity and self-esteem in every child, no matter what the child's I.Q. might be. The challenge is to fan that spark into a bright flame of light within the child and not just to hold up a light from the outside before the child's mind.

Too many children today don't think they are good enough, popular enough, smart enough, thin enough, fast enough. They lack the fundamental sense of being loved and of being lovable, and it is our mission to help them learn. Becoming a Merit Scholarship finalist, getting into a good college, winning a sports scholarship or a state championship are not one bit important unless they increase the child's sense of being loved and the child becomes more loving in return. Adults put too much value on these accomplishments for their own sake and ignore the more important value of cultivating dignity and respect for all people.

We can learn something from the four-year-old girl with the pumpkin puzzle about respect for the individual process of learning. We have to risk letting children take things apart so that they can figure out how to put them back together. The hope in all of this is that some of today's students will find new ways of putting things together that we have failed to imagine.

Jesus, lover of children, have mercy on us.

Reflection

1. What is the difference between knowledge and wisdom? Which is of greater value? How do I foster that which is more important?

2. How much competition is there in my life? Do I encourage it among my family, friends, and colleagues? Do I measure success as victory over competitors?

3. How do I build up the self-esteem of the children who are part of my life? Do I protect them from unfair expectations? Do I let them take things apart?

OUR LADY OF SORROWS

A mother bears the sorrows of her children. Their pain is her pain. There was no greater sorrow in the history of the world than the rejection and death of the Son of God. Mary carried that sorrow with her Son in faith and perseverance. Mary carried that sorrow as her share in the act of redemption; she carried it for our salvation.

This day we honor the woman who loved beyond the pain, who refused to resort to revenge or to buckle under despair, who continued to love. We honor this woman on this day by acknowledging our share in the sorrow of her Son. We pray this litany, not in the despair of guilt, but in the hope of redemption.

Litany of Repentance

Through the intercession of Mary, the woman of sorrows, we pray this prayer to you, Jesus Christ, the man of sorrows.

For our failure to choose life, defend life, and proclaim life, we ask your forgiveness. Lord, have mercy.

For our part in violence, oppression, and domination, we ask your forgiveness. Lord, have mercy.

For our share in fostering the unequal distribution of resources, we ask your forgiveness. Lord, have mercy.

For operating within systems that value profits over people, we ask your forgiveness. Lord, have mercy.

For allowing our brothers and sisters to be isolated from the love and care of community, we ask your forgiveness. Lord, have mercy.

For our intolerance of differences, we ask your forgiveness. Lord, have mercy.

For the neglect of our children, we ask your forgiveness. Lord, have mercy.

For the abandoning of our elderly, we ask your forgiveness. Lord, have mercy.

For the ignoring of our homeless, we ask your forgiveness. Lord, have mercy.

For the racism and segregation we tolerate in our society, in our churches, and in our homes, we ask your forgiveness. Lord, have mercy.

For our fear of the beatitudes and our love of efficiency, we ask your forgiveness. Lord, have mercy.

For doubting the power of love over force in settling disputes, we ask your forgiveness. Lord, have mercy.

For betraying our courage with compromise, we ask your forgiveness. Lord, have mercy.

For limiting our imaginations, we ask your forgiveness. Lord, have mercy.

For not loving our enemies, we ask your forgiveness. Lord, have mercy.

Lord Jesus Christ, from the cross you gave us your mother. May we take her into our homes to learn from her your way of suffering love. Free our hearts from the fear of loving, our feet from the fear of following, our hands from the fear of reaching out. Make us vulnerable and passionate as your mother was vulnerable and passionate. We ask this, as we ask all things, through you, our God and our Lover. Amen.

Jesus, man of sorrows, have mercy on us.

Reflection

1. Have I thanked Mary for her share in our redemption? for her compassion in our pain?

2. In the company of Our Lady of Sorrows I repent of my sins. For what do I ask forgiveness of God?

3. In the company of Our Lady of Sorrows I receive the mercy of God. How will I now show mercy?

POVERTY: DEPENDENCE ON GOD

There is nothing holy about material poverty. Poverty as deprivation of the necessities for survival is an evil that society needs to remedy. Poverty as a trap that binds people in hopelessness and despair is a killer of spirit as well as of body. Yet, since the time of Christ believers in him have embraced poverty for the kingdom of God. Those who have given up all to follow Christ have experienced the blesssings of poverty. Poverty is a paradox—it can be a burden or it can be a gift.

As gift, poverty can free us from dependence on material possessions for security. This freedom, in turn, leads to a greater freedom: freedom from the necessity of defending these possessions. When God is our source of security, we have nothing to defend, not even our lives. Poverty, when understood in this way, prepares us for the work of peace. Commitment to peacemaking comes from a conscious choice to prefer people to possessions, to live in love, and to endure evil with love rather than defend property with violence or respond to evil with revenge.

Historically, voluntary poverty has been encouraged by everyone who has seriously undertaken the work of peace— Dorothy Day, Thomas Merton, Mohandas Gandhi, Mother Teresa, Francis of Assisi, Catherine of Siena, Jesus Christ. These peace advocates were not bereft of common sense or of a practical instinct for survival. They simply lived and preached mystery on a daily basis. They understood that the basis of peace is defenselessness, which cannot exist simultaneously with material wealth. It is a hard truth to accept that the work of peace implies living a lifestyle free from the tugs and pulls of consumerism and greed. However, it is a truth that, once accepted, frees the spirit as nothing else can. It provides the only real security.

Businesses that manufacture personal security devices or provide security services are thriving these days. New locks and alarms are being invented to forestall every new tactic of crime. These devices can do everything they promise except dispel fear and insecurity. The security they offer is an illusion, the illusion that locks can give peace of mind.

The only peace we can achieve and the only security that is real are inseparable from absolute trust in Jesus Christ. As individuals, as families, and as communities of the people of God, we know that God is everything. We trust God in everything, and we act daily in this knowledge and trust. This is our source of security. We may also lock and bolt our doors, but we know that peace comes not from the locks and bolts but from our God.

On a national and global scale, it is illusion to say that we trust in God and at the same time stockpile arms for defense and money for future needs. Trust in God's material providence leads to trust in God's spiritual providence. To embrace voluntary poverty is to make a commitment to live the kingdom of God, not the kingdom of military power or the kingdom of Madison Avenue. It is necessarily to depend upon others in mutual interdependence. We are baptized to be brothers and sisters of one another. Poverty renders that relationship essential for the survival of all.

There is a Japanese proverb that says, "If you wish to do something great, go first and live among the poor." To be about God's work of peace, we must put aside distractions about possessions and their defense. The lure of the things that offer the "good life" is strong. We cannot resist casually the temptation to wealth; we need to be decisive and dramatic.

As long as we passively go along with all the trappings and benefits of materialism, we don't experience the demands of money and prestige as a problem. It is only when we resist the influence of wealth that we feel its hold on us. "If we are rich and respected it is very hard not to begin thinking of ourselves as the 'right kind' of people, and to think that therefore our way of living, of thinking, of evaluating things is the 'right way' for human beings in general. That makes us the standard, and that is pride. It is to make ourselves like God."[23]

To free ourselves from this illusion of righteousness, we must free ourselves from the material possessions that cause the illusion of prestige in the first place. The mark of the person of peace is the recognition that all people share equally in truth. None of us has a monopoly on truth; God alone is truth.

Jesus Christ accomplished the work of salvation for all while he was among the poor. He had nowhere to lay his head, he had no office, no position, and no tomb in which to be buried.

The call to voluntary poverty makes sense to those with passionate hearts who want to be like their Lord. It makes sense to those who are so in love with God that they refuse to be tied to any material thing lest it keep them from touching God. When we experience life with God in its fullness, we have no time to waste on matters that are not of God. When God enflames the fires of love in us, those fires consume all lesser desires.

God is all in all—there is no need for anything else.

Jesus, provider of all good things, have mercy on us.

Reflection

1. Have I experienced poverty as a burden? Am I afraid of poverty? Have I experienced poverty as a gift? Has it brought me freedom?

2. Would I risk violence to another in the defense of my material possessions? Is anything I own as valuable as another person's life?

3. Who are the people I consider the "right kind"? How does this judgment of mine affect what I do, with whom I associate, and where I go?

SEXUALITY AND NONVIOLENCE

With the beginning of school these days, there is often as much media coverage on the issuing of condoms in schools as on reading, writing, and arithmetic. The debate over condoms in schools centers on the children, but adults are really the problem. Our children are dealing with situations of sexual promiscuity that we have created for them.

We have given our children ambiguous messages about sexuality. On the one hand, we expect them to respect their bodies, and on the other hand, we allow their minds to be filled with a perverted image of sexuality. Movies, books, television, advertisements, dress styles, and adult behavior depict sex as a commodity to be used at will for immediate pleasure. Satisfaction is slight and passing; commitment is unimportant.

Ironically, there is a direct correlation between the increase in promiscuity and the decrease in sexual pleasure. Unfortunately, children are finding this out for themselves by becoming sexually active while very young. As a result, they seriously jeopardize their potential for sexual fulfillment as adults.

Our children deserve the best. They have been given wonderful bodies that can give them satisfaction and joy if they learn to use them as God intends them to be used. Many parents spend more time instructing their children on the use of their cars than on the use of their bodies. Bodies and emotions are a great deal more valuable and complex than cars, but we aren't stating that message very clearly by our actions.

On the contrary, we are giving the opposite message and devaluing sexuality. Casual sex and rape are so common on television that they begin to appear as a commonplace part of life. Intercourse becomes the goal of interaction between the sexes, and nothing else matters. The truth is that when two people in love commit themselves to each other, the sharing of their whole beings is expressed in intercourse, but it is not limited to that act. Their commitment and surrender enhance the physical pleasure in ways that can never be experienced by those who do not know such commitment.

Unless children witness and learn the power of sexual intimacy within an adult commitment, they will never experience the fullness of sexual pleasure. AIDS, sexually transmitted diseases, and unwanted pregnancies are not the only bad effects of misused sexuality. The worst is the loss of the sense of the power and beauty of sexuality. It is a death of the spirit, which is more pervasively harmful than testing HIV positive.

We are created to love. For some this is expressed in a physical union between two people. This is a gift from God to be cherished and used. For others, and for various reasons, the expression of love is never consummated in sexual intercourse. This does not mean that sexual love is not a part of their lives. Sexuality is not determined only by genital activity; it is part of the whole person.

We are formed by our response to love. That is what actualizes our sexual power, with or without intercourse. If we risk love, we are open to the possibility of being vulnerable to and with another person. These are aspects of sexuality that our children need to understand. They don't just need to know ways to prevent pregnancy or diseases; they need to know how to surrender and how to accept and express vulnerability. They need to understand that sharing sex with another is an act of mutual giving, not a feat to be accomplished.

Violence on dates, especially among teenagers, is growing. The increase in sexual activity among teenagers is paralleled by an increase in the violence between them. The reporting of date rapes has escalated, yet rape counselors concur that most date rapes do not get reported. Many adolescents accept violence as part of the dating process.

Among adolescents there exists a myth that romantic passion makes a sexual encounter both desirable and unavoidable. Many swallow this, but it is exactly that—a myth. The reality of human passion far exceeds the adolescent myth. Passion is an overwhelming gift of self and surrender in love to another. It requires maturity and self-restraint.

Christ's life from the Last Supper to the crucifixion is called the passion. The passion of human sexual love is related to this first, most perfect passion. Christ showed the most intense passionate love for us during his suffering. He did not feel pleasure, but he experienced passion.

Passion is like that. Sometimes it takes us beyond our capabilities. Passion is abandonment to the other and free surrender for the other without regard for self. At times the surrender is pleasurable and satisfying, at times it is demanding and self-sacrificing.

Our children learn from us; they have not learned good sexuality because we are not willing to put the time and tenderness into our own sexuality that it deserves. We are all responsible for developing our sexuality, no matter the vocation or lifestyle we live. This responsibility involves risk and a commitment to God and to ourselves, as well as to each other.

Many married people have not made this commitment wholeheartedly, and their uninteresting sex lives reflect it. Good sex doesn't come with marriage vows; it is like anything else in marriage—a gift to be discovered and cherished and appreciated in the process of mutual self-giving. Any married person will vouch for the fact that the way a husband and wife treat each other all day long will be reflected in the way they treat each other in their times of intimacy.

Jesus Christ lived and died a celibate. No one has better understood human sexuality or lived it more passionately than Jesus. He opened his heart to us, offering his vulnerable spirit to the risk of rejection and abuse. From those who denied him he experienced betrayal and rejection. But Jesus also offered his vulnerable spirit and body to the possibility of love. From those who believed he received love and commitment.

We learn all things from Jesus. We learn love. We learn passion. We learn to treasure every gift of body and spirit that we have received so that we may live fully the passion of love for which we are created. When we live this way of committed love and mutual self-giving, our children will grow in an environment that can foster healthy and holy sexual development. They will still have to make their own choices and decisions, but they will have a foundation on which to build and a standard from which to choose.

Jesus, intimate friend, have mercy on us.

Reflection

1. Is there passion in my life? Do I value my sexuality? How do I show this in my behavior? my entertainment? my dress? my language?

2. Am I vulnerable to another person? to God? How do I give flesh to this vulnerability to the other? to God?

3. What is the difference between only seeking pleasure in sexual encounters and offering oneself sexually to another in committed love? Does commitment decrease or increase sexual pleasure?

OCTOBER TO DECEMBER:
INTRODUCTION

Jesus, Priest most high, offer us as living sacrifices to God.

October

By baptism we are brought into the priesthood of Christ. We share ministry with Christ the Priest. We share in the offering of our bodies with Christ's for the love of our brothers and sisters, and we share in the transformation of our beings with Christ's for the redemption of the world. Priesthood does not give us political, economic, or social power, but it does give us the power of love, which is the only power that will endure and ultimately reign.

Jesus showed us the essence of priesthood, which is the willingness to endure evil with love rather than respond to evil with violence. In this century Mohandas Gandhi understood this message of Jesus clearly and practiced it faithfully. Gandhi was not a Christian, but he based his life on the Sermon on the Mount. He made his life an offering that pointed to the truth of Christ's message: the infinite truth rooted in love. *Jesus, eternal truth of God, offer us as living sacrifices to God.*

Christianity has not always been consistent in measuring its standards of action by the standards of Christ. For seventeen centuries we have justified war and created feasts to celebrate military victories. We have misinterpreted the message of God and have misused the things of God. The Feast of the

Holy Rosary originated as the celebration of a naval victory—
that is a misuse of the things of God. We try to return to the
purity of our original devotion to the rosary, and we ask Mary
to be with us in our search for truth in our prayer, the truth
of enduring love in union with the Lamb of God. *Jesus, standard of devotions, offer us as living sacrifices to God.*

Holy men and women of the past personified priesthood
made flesh. They lived it faithfully and showed us by their
lives how to mediate the grace of Christ to the world by offering
their lives with his to the Father. They showed us how to intercede by offering their bodies as living sacrifices in life as
well as in death. This offering was for them an experience
of priesthood, and it is the experience to which they invite
us. *Jesus, intercessor for peace, offer us as living sacrifices to God.*

Priesthood is not exercised only in churches. The priesthood of Jesus is a ministry exercised in the streets to those
who never make it to the inside of a respectable church. The
Good Shepherd went to those sheep that were lost. He offered
himself to them and for them. In our time some of those lost
sheep are without homes and the basic necessities of life. Children are growing up in shelters or on streets. Their roots have
no nourishment; they need someone to lead them to water.
Jesus, priest of the streets, offer us as living sacrifices to God.

November

It is possible for ordinary people to become holy; that is
the mystery of a religion based on the incarnation of God in
human flesh. Jesus Christ became one of us to unite us with
himself. In this union is our holiness. On the Feast of All Saints
we celebrate the extraordinary holiness of those people who
lived this union in ordinary ways and now live it ecstatically
for all eternity. *Jesus, holiness of the saints, offer us as living sacrifices
to God.*

Even though the purpose of priesthood is to form community, sometimes the priest must be the one who stands apart

to show the way to God. St. Martin of Tours had to step from the crowd at a crucial point in his life. He had to choose the way of Jesus, the way of love of enemies over the way of the state, the way of destruction of enemies. This choice entailed the offering of his life. *Jesus, courage of Christians, offer us as living sacrifices to God.*

What Martin did in the fourth century, Dorothy Day did in our times. She stepped from the crowd and spoke the truth of the beatitudes with all the passion of her being. From the pulpit of the Bowery slums, in clothes cast aside by someone else, Dorothy held up to us all the clarity of the gospel call of justice and peace. *Jesus, activist for justice, offer us as living sacrifices to God.*

Some people are activists for justice just by their presence. Their beings are songs of praise and worship. Their bodies are the incense of their evening offering. In them God is glorified; to them we are grateful. They teach us the meaning of Thanksgiving. *Jesus, pure of heart, offer us as living sacrifices to God.*

December

In no one do we see purity of heart more clearly than in Mary. Desire, vulnerability, single-heartedness, receptivity, surrender, and passion combined in Mary to form a perfect vessel for her Son and her Lord. Like him, Mary reflects the mercy of God. To be centered on God as Mary was impels us to be actively involved in God's works of mercy. We learn the mercy of God in the loving arms of Mary. *Jesus, heart of mercy, offer us as living sacrifices to God.*

We come to Mary at Christmas to ask her to help us teach our children the purity of heart that she embodied. We ask her to help us prepare our children to understand the celebration of the birth of Christ. All the festivities of the season ought to be consistent with the person of the season, Jesus Christ. We pray for the courage to be faithful to the meaning of Christ's birth in every detail of our holiday celebrations. *Jesus, teacher of peace, offer us as living sacrifices to God.*

October 2

MOHANDAS K. GANDHI

October 2, 1869, was the birthday of Mohandas Karam-
chand Gandhi. He stands apart as the great disciple and
teacher of nonviolence for this century. He was a faithful
Hindu ascetic who based his philosophy on the Sermon on
the Mount. As Christians who try to base our lives on the
Sermon on the Mount, we could profit from looking more
deeply at this simple man of God.

The picture of a little man in homespun clothes meeting
with the leaders of the British government might invite com-
parisons with David and Goliath. However, a less than cur-
sory glance reveals that the giant is really the Mahatma, "the
Great Soul," a title affectionately given Gandhi by his own
people. It would take more than an empire to topple the truth
of the man.

Gandhi's emphasis was on the absence of fear and the presence of love in the service of truth. Fear causes defenses, conflicts, and eventually wars. People are afraid of losing their
property. They fear physical danger, they fear themselves,
they fear the different and the unknown. Men and women
purchase weapons, build walls, and defend themselves against
all their fears. But no matter how high the wall, it never seems
tall enough. Fear becomes a mountain that is always a little
higher than the mountain of defenses. And so they keep building. And so we keep building.

Gandhi, sounding like St. Paul, broke down the mountain of fear with love. "Do not let fear lead you to build up defences against others. Rid yourself of fear; that is the place to begin. Then make yourself defenceless, in the usual sense of that term."[24] Love is the only cure for fear. We don't fear people at the same time we are loving them.

The love of which Gandhi spoke is not easy or sentimental; it is difficult, rooted in God yet grounded in reality. It is the ability to desire only the good, to assume suffering rather than inflict it, to serve without caring for recognition or response.

The similarity between Gandhi's teachings and those of the New Testament should be obvious. Gandhi recognized the power of Jesus' message of love. "Jesus lived and died in vain if he did not teach us to regulate the whole of life by the eternal law of love."[25] Gandhi recognized Jesus' willingness to suffer for the sake of love. In Jesus an infinite capacity to love was matched by an infinite willingness to suffer.

Gandhi understood redemptive suffering. Personal efforts to divest himself of fear and to embrace a suffering love were Gandhi's stepping stones to truth. Truth was the rock upon which his philosophy was built. There was not a word in his native language to express Gandhi's ideal, so he coined one: *Satyagraha,* "truth force."

To understand Satyagraha, we must approach it reverently, as we would a religious symbol. It is not merely a tool of revolution to be taught to the masses. For Gandhi, God was truth and truth was God. Satyagraha is the search for the sacred; it is "not the means of achieving unity but the fruit of inner unity already achieved."[26] Satyagraha is the lifelong effort to disarm the heart of all hatred. One who enters into this effort must be prepared to suffer. An understanding of this ideal of Satyagraha is essential for a basic knowledge of nonviolence.

Gandhi was a person who actively sought out the truth in any situation. If truth was being denied or compromised, he took action. He taught us to actively resist whatever evil or untruth is present with a heart free of hatred and open to suffering. The loving and willing acceptance of suffering in the search for truth is beyond human capabilities; therefore, the root of Satyagraha is prayer. "My greatest weapon is mute prayer."[27]

Too often people equate nonviolence with non-action. Gandhi certainly put that misconception to rest. "Nonviolence, as I understand it, is the most active force in the world. . . . During my half a century of experience I have not yet come across a situation when I had to say that I was helpless, that I had no remedy in terms of nonviolence."[28] These words are from a man who lived through the racism of South Africa, the oppression of colonial India and the horrors of World Wars I and II.

As we commemorate the birthday of Mohandas Gandhi, we stand with billions of dollars of weapons poised for use whenever we feel threatened. We are consumed by violence in families and neighborhoods and nations.

It will do us good to pause and remember a man at whose death almost every flag in the world was lowered. It will do us good to remember a man who clung to nothing and gained freedom for a nation. It will do us good to remember a man who risked his life in witness to his belief in the goodness of humanity and the infinite love of God. Mohandas Gandhi, pray for us!

Jesus, eternal truth of God, offer us as living sacrifices to God.

Reflection

1. Do I know the teachings of the Sermon on the Mount? Do I base my life on those teachings?

2. Is there any place in my life where I think truth is being compromised? Why? What would Jesus do? What can I do?

3. Is there a mountain of fear around me? Is there anyway I can lower it? What fears can I release? Where is God in all this?

October 7

OUR LADY OF THE ROSARY

Christianity has not always been consistent in following
the example of Christ. War and the justification of war are
probably our most glaring departures from the message of
Jesus to love our enemies. In the past century most wars have
been fought by Christians against Christians, with both sides
claiming to be doing the work of God. Not only are the wars
fought "in the name of God," but battles are commemorated
with religious feasts and blessings. God is further blasphemed
when victory is claimed through God's intercession.

Plenary indulgences were first granted at the time of the
Crusades for the slaying of a Muslim. Catholic men and
women from the United States were encouraged to fight in
World War II "for God and country." All the branches of
the services, including the crews that dropped the atomic
bombs, had the services of Catholic chaplains. Planes and
bombs are blessed. On the other side, Catholic men and
women from Germany were also fighting for faith and father-
land. The belt buckle of the German army uniform carried
the inscription "God is with us."

Today submarines carrying first-strike nuclear missles are
given Christian names and blessed by priests. The troops are
blessed, the flags are flown in the churches, patriotic songs
are sung at Mass. There are posters of Christ in front of a
national flag, of Mary carrying the infant Christ, who is hold-

ing a grenade, of Mary and the Church surrounded by war-
planes. Blasphemy upon blasphemy. Not only is evil done,
but it is portrayed as good, the work of God.

The Feast of Our Lady of the Rosary is an example of
the misuse of religion for political purposes. Pope Pius V in-
augurated the feast to celebrate the naval victory of Lepanto,
claiming that Mary had interceded with God for the destruction of the enemy. Can we imagine Mary ever petitioning
God for the death and destruction of children of God? Victory in battle does not mean that one side gets more points
than the other; it means perhaps that one side gets fewer
casualties than the other. It means that more people on one
side die than on the other. To pray for victory is to pray for
the death of the enemy. This is contrary to Christ's impera-
tive to love one's enemies.

Does this tainted origin of the Feast of Our Lady of the
Rosary imply that the rosary is not important or that the praying of the rosary is not valid? Of course not. It just means that
we must be cautious not to use the things of God for the purposes of Caesar.[29] The rosary, which long preceded the battle
of Lepanto, has always been a powerful prayer in the tradition of the people of God. Something in us responds to a simple
reminder of the presence of God in our lives. Something in us
needs to have a visible, tactile reminder of this presence as we
go through our days.

There is nothing superstitious about the beads. They are
simply a reminder of the constant call of the human heart to
God and of the response of God to that call. The use of prayer
beads predates Christianity. They were used as a reminder
of God, not a guarantee of holiness. We wear wedding rings
to remind us of the one to whom we are bound in love. The
ring does not make the marriage happy, and the beads do
not make the person holy.

It has taken many centuries for the rosary as we know it
today to evolve. Originally it was a way of praying for those
who could not recite the 150 psalms. Fifteen decades of the
rosary add up to 150 beads. While we are praying the numer-

ous Hail Marys, our attention is focused on events in the life of Christ that are referred to as the "mysteries."

The rosary is a prayer that crosses economic and social classes and national boundaries. Kings and beggars, children and old people, the simple-minded and the intelligent finger the beads. Rosary beads can be made of gold-strung gems or knotted string—the material doesn't matter. In times of persecution in Ireland, farmers used to keep ten pebbles in their pockets and move them from one pocket to another as they prayed their rosary.

As the rosary becomes part of daily life, it creates a rhythm. It is the rhythm of constantly holding before our minds and hearts pictures and words from the life of Christ. Our hope is that the rhythm will become part of our own lives to such a degree that our lives will reflect the same words and pictures. It is good for the human heart to bend, for the body to kneel, for the hand to move along the beads, for us to meet Christ in the company of his mother.

Jesus, standard of devotions, offer us as living sacrifices to God.

Reflection

1. Can I imagine Mary petitioning God for the death and destruction of children of God? Have I ever prayed for victory in war?

2. Do I pray the rosary? Do I have a sense of the rhythm of Christ's life meshing with mine?

3. Are there ways in which Christianity in practice is inconsistent with the teachings of Jesus? Are there any ways in which my life is inconsistent with the teachings of Jesus?

HOLY MEN AND WOMEN: INTERCESSORS FOR PEACE

In the Church's liturgical year, October has the most feasts of great men and women. It is the month of Thérèse of Lisieux and Teresa of Avila, renewers of religious orders; of Luke, Simon, and Jude, apostles of Jesus and leaders of the first Christian community; of Bruno and Paul of the Cross, founders of religious communities; of Francis, the poor man of Assisi; of Margaret Mary Alocoque, one to whom Jesus revealed his heart; of Ignatius of Antioch and the North American Jesuit martyrs, men spanning distant centuries, chosen to sow the seed of God in new lands with their blood.

To celebrate the lives of these people of God is to make an act of faith in the priesthood of Christ. All these witnesses lived their priesthood with passion and zeal. By doing so, they lived out the mystery of redemption. They shared in Christ's work of gathering the people of God into community for the praise and glory of God and for the spread of the kingdom of God on this earth.

We also are called to assume the responsibility of priesthood in this company of saints. At baptism every Christian is consecrated to share in the priesthood of Christ. This sacrament gives us the gift of being one with Christ, the one High Priest, and the responsibility of sharing this priesthood with him and with each other.

Our role as priests is to form community, to assemble in union with Christ as the people of God, to offer ourselves and all the world to be transformed. In our priesthood we share intimately in Christ's offering of himself to the Father. We mediate the grace of this offering to one another. From the depths of our being we become intercessors before God for the people of God.

The saints we celebrate this month assumed their baptismal role as priests with Christ and became intercessors for all of us. We have not received a lesser call than these saints; our response ought not to be any less than theirs. For most of us, the very thought of being like such people makes us uncomfortable. After all, those people were mystics and martyrs; they had visions and ecstasies and special vocations; they changed the face of their times and ours. We're not in the same league. We can't be expected to live as freely and as passionately as these saints did.

Because of our baptism, not only are we expected to live like the saints but we are given the grace to do so. One of the reasons we focus on the lives of the saints is to learn from them how to be like Christ. We learn what helped these people to remain faithful to their call to be "other Christs." We learn what united them with one another and with their God, and what unites them with us.

The thread that joined all these men and women together was their willingness to stand apart from their own society and to share in the redemption of their times. They prayed to know their God and they stood by their God, no matter the cost, not out of heroism but out of love. They knew Christ intimately, and that knowledge formed compassionate hearts open to others. These men and women cared so much for their brothers and sisters who were suffering from the effects of sin that they offered their bodies as living sacrifices. This offering was for them an experience of priesthood.

The thread that unites these saints with us is the priesthood of Christ. As Priest, Christ offered once and for all the sacrifice of redemption for all peoples, past, present, and future. Neither the saints nor we can add to the priesthood of Christ. It is complete and perfect in itself. But by sharing in it we participate in making Christ's offering present in our day as the saints made it present in their day.

Like the holy men and women whose feasts we celebrate this month, we are to be "other priests" in Christ. Christ made peace with God for us; we are called to make peace with God for one another, that is, we are called to be intercessors for this peace. Intercessors do not just pray for peace; they unite with Christ the Priest, who offers himself for others. The priest is one who offers the victim to God. Christ was himself both Victim and Priest. Only Christ is the perfect Victim and the most high Priest, but we are brought into the mystery as people both offered and offering. When the mystery of Christ's suffering joins the mystery of our suffering, priesthood is lived.

Mysticism, ecstasy, and extraordinary religious phenomena were not the characteristics that made the saints holy. Such experiences were unique gifts that had a purpose and a great cost. What made the saints holy was their union with the Holy. Saints are people who cannot be satisfied with less than the best. They embraced the passion of God and the priesthood of Christ for what they were: unlimited, alive, and all-consuming. With that embrace ordinary men and women became passionate people who redeemed their times.

Our day is no less demanding than the past; there is no less a need for redemption and hope. Some would say that we have more need for the peace of Christ than ever before. If so, we have more need than ever before to hear the call to priesthood, to accept the vocation of mediation and intercession for the people of God.

We pray that this call will be heard in our time. We pray that we will understand and accept the fullness of priesthood. We pray that we will desire to be one with Christ the Priest as he gives his life in love. It is no small feat to be willing to give up one's life for another; it is greater than visions and revelations. Receiving the stigmata and having ecstasies pale in comparison. It is the surrendering of ourselves in love that is the essential. To this we have been called.

Jesus, intercessor for peace, offer us as living sacrifices to God.

Reflection

1. How do I live my baptismal call to priesthood? How do I form community for the spread of the kingdom? How do I offer sacrifice for the redemption of the world?

2. Which saints am I attracted to? Why? How do they act as intercessors for me?

3. Am I called to know Christ intimately? Am I called to be a saint? Am I called to be an intercessor for peace?

HOMELESSNESS: A CHALLENGE FOR CHRISTIANS

October is a changeable friend. October can be summer to us when a warm sunny day allows us to shed our sweaters and wear sandals one more time. Even a swim in the ocean is possible sometimes when the water still has its summer warmth.

October can be winter when its cold wind brings out coats and hats before their due time. Storm windows are put on to block out the open screens, and the furnace kicks on for the first time.

October can be its glorious fall self when it chooses. Trees shamelessly flaunt bright-colored clothes as they dance in the wind for any who will notice. The ground toughens itself against the impending winter. We feel its hardness under our feet, as if it wants to help us be sturdier for the months ahead. All the animals are scurrying around storing and burrowing. The birds are leaving for places with longer days and warmer winds. No sunny day can fool them into thinking spring.

October somehow never teases us into thinking of spring. Reality is too honest for that deception. Pods, not buds, are on the tree branches. The most playfully oblivious among us know the cold and the darkness that are around the corner.

None sense this more keenly than the homeless. The severity of winter for them means more than higher fuel bills and snow to shovel. For them it can mean life or death. Survival is more difficult in winter for those who live on the streets or who move from shelter to shelter suffering from the great disease of rootlessness. Plants die if they are uprooted too many times. So do people.

Our economy has created homeless people in staggering numbers. There are people with jobs who cannot afford to rent an apartment. Entire families live in their cars, on the streets, or in shelters. Mentally ill people who should have continual assistance are on their own. In some cases they have the money but not the ability to care for themselves. A significant number of veterans are on the streets still fighting the wars that destroyed them. Teenagers running from unsafe homes fill the alleys and street corners.

No Christian is exempt from giving a response to this great tragedy of homelessness. It is not only the responsibility of those people who staff the soup kitchens and shelters, or of the priests and parishioners of those inner-city churches that open their doors to the homeless all winter. It is not only the responsibility of those who see homeless persons on their stoops or at their subway stop. We all must see and we all must refuse to stop seeing. We cannot let ourselves be overwhelmed by the numbers. We do not treat homelessness by the thousands and millions; we treat homelessness as it is suffered— one by one.

In a first-grade classroom in New York City, a teacher used to teach her students a new vocabulary to use when referring to the homeless. The children would talk about the "bum" or the "bag lady" they saw on the way to school or on the school steps. Patiently and compassionately, the teacher taught the children to call these people "poor unfortunate gentlemen" or "poor unfortunate ladies." The children would proudly repeat the big words and would go home and tell about the new way they had learned to talk about people who lived on the street. This teacher taught dignity and mercy by her words, not sympathy or self-righteousness. She taught the children to be careful but also to be kind.

The children learned. Children learn well when they are taught well. One day little Emily pulled her teacher aside and told her about the "Lamstons Lady." Lamstons was a five-and-ten-cent store on the corner, and a homeless woman huddled in its doorway every night for protection and warmth. The woman was still there and beginning to move about when the children passed her on the way to school. Emily whispered to her teacher, "I give her a nickel when I have one." The child was poor; a nickel was a treasure to her.

Emily's nickel, given in love, was the Christian response of a six-year-old to homelessness. Our responses as adults will be as varied as our talents and abilities. It must always be more than just money given begrudgingly to a persistent beggar. Some of us will open our doors and provide food and beds; some will work to change the systems that cause homelessness; some will financially support the works of mercy; some will provide employment; some will assist those addicted to drugs. And all of us will pray for hearts open to conversion, to living the compassion of Christ.

"For I was hungry and you gave me food, I was thirsty and you gave me something to drink, I was a stranger and you welcomed me, I was naked and you gave me clothing, I was sick and you took care of me, I was in prison and you visited me" (Matthew 25:35-36). We will be judged on our love for one another. "Truly I tell you, just as you did it to one of the least of these who are members of my family, you did it to me" (Matthew 25:40).

Jesus, Priest of the streets, offer us as living sacrifices to God.

Reflection

1. Where is the shelter closest to me? Where is the nearest soup kitchen? Have I worked inside either of them? Would Christ be working there? Should I?

2. Am I afraid of or embarrassed by the homeless people I meet on the street? Do I look at their faces and see my brothers and sisters? Do I look the other way or cross the street to avoid them?

3. When I am thirsty, do you give me to drink? When hungry, do you feed me? When naked, do you clothe me? When in prison, do you visit me? When a stranger, do you welcome me?

November 1

ALL SAINTS DAY

The most improbable act of God was the incarnation of Jesus Christ. God became human. Two thousand years of Christianity have left us almost indifferent to this reality. Perhaps we think of Jesus as one of us but not fully divine. Or we think of Jesus as God but not fully human. Or perhaps we realize that Jesus is God and man but not how radically he has united us to himself in grace. We cannot fathom the fullness of life God offers us—a fullness both human and divine. We doubt that God can share divinity with us in such fullness.

To think this way is to limit our faith to what we can comprehend. The incarnation of Jesus calls us beyond our limitations. By faith we enter into the mystery of Jesus' intimacy with his Father and our intimacy with Jesus. We enter into the mystery of the possibility of holiness for ordinary people because of the holiness of God made flesh in Jesus.

Today, the Feast of All Saints, we celebrate the lives of all those people of God who, because they believed in this mystery, now live in it for all eternity. We celebrate those people of every age and of every culture who fell in love with God in Jesus Christ. Within this love they themselves became one with God, and so they themselves became holy.

Together with people all over the world, we celebrate today men and women whose lives bore witness to the message of Jesus. We celebrate Martin of Tours and Paul Miki, Thérèse of Lisieux and Maria Goretti, John the Baptist and Joseph of Nazareth. We anticipate the Church's declaration of the holiness of Archbishop Oscar Romero and Dorothy Day, Takashi Nagai and Edith Stein. We celebrate those holy people of other faiths who may never be canonized in the Catholic faith but whom we count among the blessed: Mohandas Gandhi, Martin Luther King, Jr., and Etty Hillesum.

Since there are only a limited number of days in a year, it is impossible to have a feast for every one of these holy people, so today we honor them all. A lengthy and expensive process of canonization is not always necessary for us to accept that someone is with God, that someone is a saint. This is the day also for our own personal saints, for those holy people who have gone before us, those whom we have known and loved on this earth. We need to name these people as a way of keeping alive the history of the Church and the history of salvation. We need to reflect on these people and their lives of service and fidelity. Christianity depends upon the people of God to spread the word of God from one person to another. It depends upon every Christian to spread this word, not just the few who get written up in the history books.

Fr. Martin Jenco, a priest who spent 564 days as a hostage in Lebanon, told the story of his personal litany of saints after his release. During the five months he spent in solitary confinement, Father Jenco thought and prayed about many things. One of the ways he prayed during this time was to name in gratitude the people he had known who were messengers of God to him. Beginning with his parents, he went through all his saints and prayed to them.

We do not have to be in solitary confinement to pray this way. This is the day to celebrate all our saints who now live with God in all the fullness of God. They spoke to us of God with their lives when they were among us, and now that they are with God we ask them to speak to God for us still.

Catholic churches ordinarily have some statues of saints in them. Our Church is unique in this practice. It is a wonderful tribute to the presence of Jesus among us as a man. Because of Jesus we are all called to sanctity. The statues in our homes and churches are images of men and women, rich and poor, young and old, recent and distant in time. The Incarnation forever prohibits any limitations on who is called to holiness.

We are all called. Every saint also sinned. Some were as notorious in their sins as in their sanctity. God is God, and the most hardened sinner can be converted. Our consciousness of saints does not distract us from God but shows us the way to God. Devotion to the saints keeps us conscious that there are multiple ways to bring God the scent of jasmine.

Saints have offered to God the perfume of their lives from prisons and monasteries, from businesses and homes, from large cities and rural towns, from hospital beds and concentration camps. The aroma of their example fills us until, like our saints, we become the aroma of Christ.

Jesus, holiness of the saints, offer us as living sacrifices to God.

Reflection

1. What does the incarnation of God in Christ mean to me? What does Jesus' humanity mean to me? What does my share in Jesus' divinity mean to me?

2. Can I make a litany of saints? Am I able to share this with someone else? Will I be in someone else's litany?

3. Do I teach my children about the saints? When was the last time I bought a book on the life of a saint for a child? When was the last time I gave a child a religious gift?

ST. MARTIN OF TOURS

So often the history of the Church is given in terms of councils of the Church or eras of Christianity. For example, we speak of pre-Vatican II and post-Vatican II or pre-Trent and post-Trent. In a similar way the world's history is divided according to wars or the reigns of monarchs. Both ways of reporting the events of the times often miss the people of those times, especially the people who were out of step with the times. The prophets of every age never fit the general descriptions of their contemporaries.

On November 11 we celebrate the Feast of St. Martin of Tours. Martin was a man who did not fit the times in which he lived. In the fourth century, when Christians were joining the army of Rome in large numbers, Martin refused to serve. This century is usually noted as the time when Constantine made Christianity the religion of the state and when Ambrose and Augustine introduced the just war theory. It was also the time of Martin.

Martin was born of pagan parents in the country that is now Hungary. His father served in the military, and Martin himself was inducted into the service at the age of fifteen. When he was eighteen, Martin became a catechumen and began the study of the Christian faith with the intention of becoming a Christian. A few years after his baptism, Martin gave up his commission and requested dismissal from the army because of his desire to follow the ways of Christ.

We would say today that what Martin did was file for conscientious objector status. This is always more difficult to do when one is already commissioned in the military; it exposes the man or woman to abuse and ridicule at the hands of other members of the service. Martin's decision was not accepted any more easily then than it would be now. But his reasons were clear, "I am a soldier of Christ and it is not lawful for me to fight."

At the time of the Persian Gulf War, over two thousand men and women in the armed forces of the United States filed for conscientious objector status because they did not believe in the war. Like Martin, they were accused of changing their minds, of being cowards, of being unpatriotic. Thirty-five of them were imprisoned, and twelve were still incarcerated two years later. And this is in a country that officially recognizes the rights of its citizens not to fight against their consciences.

Martin objected to killing on the basis of his understanding of Christianity. After his conversion he measured all his actions according to the standards of Christ. War was not compatible with love of enemies. Martin had the courage to stand by his conversion when his decision was unpopular.

As Christians, we must measure all the actions of our lives according to the standards of Christ. We must have the courage to listen to our consciences no matter the cost. Lack of understanding or acceptance from others is of no consequence. We will feel the pain of rejection or ridicule, but that is of no consequence. The way of Christ is the way of all Christians. Nothing else is of any consequence.

Jesus, courage of Christians, offer us as living sacrifices to God.

Reflection

1. What did Martin of Tours mean when he said, "I am a soldier of Christ and it is not lawful for me to fight"? Do I consider conscientious objectors to be cowards?

2. What was my feeling when the Persian Gulf War was in operation? What is my feeling now? Do I trust the military to tell the truth? How do my standards measure up against the standards of Jesus with regard to war?

3. When was the last time I followed my conscience and it cost me something? Was it worth it? How did it affect future decisions?

November 29

DOROTHY DAY

On November 8, 1897, Dorothy Day was born in Brooklyn, New York. On November 29, 1980, Dorothy Day died in the Bowery section of New York City. Only a bridge separates those two boroughs of New York.

Dorothy's life was in itself a bridge connecting the homeless with a safe shelter, the workers with their rights, the young with a vision for a different future based on cooperation rather than competition, the Catholic of today's comfortable Church with the radical message of the Sermon on the Mount.

As I write I have two recollections of events that reflect Dorothy's simplicity and her ordinariness. The first took place in Chicago in the early seventies. Dorothy was receiving an award from DePaul University for her service to the poor. To the small crowd gathered to hear her, Dorothy spoke not of her own work or even of the Catholic Worker movement but of St. Vincent de Paul; she made him present in that room. Those of us listening felt as if St. Vincent was a close friend of Dorothy's, someone she had just left in New York. She had a way of sharing her experience of living with the great saints of the past that made the communion of saints real and vibrant.

On that night in Chicago, Vincent de Paul was with us in his care for the poor, the street people of his day. We left knowing that we had to do the same, not because Dorothy aroused us to do it, but because she faced us with the truth

of the gospel call. Truth rooted in the gospel was her foundation. For Dorothy, the gospel was sufficient reason to move
her to action. To listen to her was to feel the same motiva-
tion and the same sense of urgency to respond.

The second image I carry of Dorothy was ten years later,
only a year before her death. She was sitting at a table in
Maryhouse, a Catholic Worker house in New York. It was
Friday night and we were gathered for a meeting. These Fri-
day night meetings have been a tradition in the Catholic
Worker movement since its inception. They provide the op-
portunity for discussion and clarification of thought. Fr. Daniel
Berrigan calls them the "greatest free university in the world."

That evening there was a performance of religious music.
Looking very much like an elderly poor woman, Dorothy
smiled and rocked a little to the music as she listened. She
wore a plain cotton dress from the poor box; her white hair
was braided like a crown on her head, and around it was
wrapped a simple scarf. I sat at the other end of the table,
thinking that across from me was probably the most influen-
tial American Catholic of our century. She sat unattended
in a poor house in the worst section of a large city slum—
how like the Man to whom she had given her life, the Man
who lived in similar circumstances two thousand years ago.
Sanctity is expressed in very ordinary ways!

Who was this woman who had such an influence on our
Church? Dorothy came from a family that traveled a great
deal in order for her journalist father to get work. They practiced no religion, so Dorothy grew up with a smattering of
knowledge of God and the saints gleaned from her neighbors
in the crowded tenements of Chicago and New York.

As a young adult she followed her father's inclinations and
took up a career in journalism, settling in New York and as-
sociating with the liberal, free-thinking writers and artists of
Greenwich Village. Like many of them, Dorothy was an athe-
ist. Like many of them, Dorothy was concerned about the
rights of workers. She wrote for the socialist paper *The Daily
Worker*.

Dorothy was a thinker, a reader, a writer, and an activist for human rights. As a pacifist, she opposed all wars. In her twenties Dorothy had a year-long affair with a man in Europe, and she also had an abortion. After that relationship had ended, Dorothy entered into a common-law marriage with a man in New York. This man was to be the father of her daughter Tamara.

It was Tamara's birth that brought Dorothy to God. She wanted her child to know God, so she had Tamara baptized and began the process of instruction for her own entrance into the Church. This conversion began her lifetime commitment to Jesus and to the radical call of the gospel. It was the beginning of her constant fidelity to the Church.

In partnership with Peter Maurin, a French peasant and philosopher, Dorothy launched her long career of Catholic social action. Together they founded the Catholic Worker movement and began the publication of *The Catholic Worker,* a paper that still sells for a penny a copy. The Catholic Worker movement speaks a clear and consistent message: Open your door to the poor, feed them, clothe them, live with them, be poor with them as Christ was. Love all people, say no to all forms of violence and killing at all times and in all circumstances. There are no exceptions to the gospel call to love one another.

Dorothy's power was not in her written words, as eloquent as they were, but in her living words, her example of love in action. As mentor to peacemakers and prophets, Dorothy guided and prodded her Church into faithfulness to the call of Jesus to love unconditionally.

By her bedside all her life was the New Testament. Dorothy prayed always. She read the great saints and scholars of our faith and became friends with them. Mass was her daily nourishment and the source of her strength and passion. She prayed the rosary, made silent retreats, fasted, and did all things in imitation of her Lord.

Dorothy never looked for success and taught her followers not to look for it either. Dorothy was of God, for God, and with God, and nothing else mattered. She lived a little way

among the little people, in the same way that Thérèse of
Lisieux lived a little way. Both women have turned the world
upside down with hope and life. Their little way is the lever
that moves heaven and earth. Their way is the way of the
cross. Neither feared to embrace it for the love of their God
and their brothers and sisters.

> When we have spiritual reading at meals, when we have
> the rosary at night, when we have study groups, forums,
> when we go out to distribute literature at meetings, or sell
> it on street corners, Christ is there with us. What we do
> is very little, but it is like the little boy with a few loaves
> and fishes. Christ took that little and increased it. He will
> do the rest. What we do is so little we may seem to be con-
> stantly failing. But so did he fail. He met with apparent
> failure on the Cross. But unless the seed fall into the earth
> and die, there is no harvest. And why must we see results?
> Our work is to sow. Another generation will be reaping
> the harvest.[30]

All you holy men and women of God, praise the Lord.
All you peacemakers and earth movers, praise the Lord.
All you lovers of the poor and homeless, praise the Lord.
All you prophets of the Beatitudes, praise the Lord.
All you courageous and faithful disciples, praise the Lord.
All you holy friends, crowned with whitened braids, cotton
    scarves and eternal life, praise the Lord.

Thank you, Dorothy! Thank you, God, for Dorothy!

Jesus, activist for justice, offer us as living sacrifices to God.

Reflection

1. Consider Dorothy Day's daily rhythm of Mass, rosary,
reading the Gospels, and service to the poor. Are these activities related and necessary to each other? Are these activities present in my life?

2. Dorothy Day, a lay woman, made a week-long silent retreat every year. Is that extreme? What does giving time to a retreat say? Can I make a retreat?

3. Do I offer my few loaves and fishes to Christ? Do I believe that Christ will accept them and bless them and use them to feed the world?

THANKSGIVING

Thirty years ago at a state hospital in a large city, I met Douglas. Douglas was thirteen. He had been in a wheelchair in the same institution since birth. Actually Douglas was tied in the chair to prevent his falling.

Douglas had very little motor control. He could move his hands and upper body slightly, not enough to push his own chair. He could hold his head up, but it took so much effort that often when he was tired, he would just let it rest on his shoulder. Douglas had difficulty talking because of the weakness of the muscles in his mouth. His speech was slow and garbled at times.

Douglas seemed to have a clear mind and thought long thoughts. Over time he managed to tell me, without self-pity or resentment, that he had been left at the hospital at birth. Nurses verified this fact. Douglas had not had a visit from anyone in the entire thirteen years he was hospitalized. He had never seen his parents. He had no ties outside the hospital. All his earthly possessions fit into a little sack that hung on the back of his wheelchair.

On Sundays Douglas and I and eight other wheelchair-bound boys used to go over to another building on the property for Mass. Older men who usually used walkers pushed the boys' chairs. We went in all kinds of weather; it was always an excited and eager entrance procession.

One particular Sunday torrential rain prevented our excursion. The boys were disappointed. I tried to explain that we didn't have to go to the other building to meet God. God was with us and among us, and we could talk to God whenever we wanted to.

Douglas interrupted in his slow, slurred speech, "I know."

I asked what he meant. He answered laboriously, "I talk to God every night."

The other boys and I were straining to understand this boy who seemed so confident of what he was saying. I asked, "What do you say every night?"

Douglas held his head up straight, gave us a beautiful smile, and replied in a clear voice, "I say thank you."

Jesus, pure of heart, offer us as living sacrifices to God.

Reflection

1. Am I as dependent on God as Douglas was?

2. Can I kneel this night in the presence of God and say, "Thank you"?

3. Is there a person like Douglas in my life? Do I appreciate him or her? Do I bless God for him or her?

December 12

OUR LADY OF GUADALUPE

When I was a child growing up in a Catholic family and a student attending Catholic schools, I heard the stories of Fatima and Lourdes and Knock. To a child those places seemed far away. I used to wonder if the Mother of God would ever come to someone in America. It was only as an adult that I heard of Our Lady of Guadalupe. Mary did come to someone in America long before her better-known European apparitions. But the story of Guadalupe is unknown to many Americans.

On December 9, 1531, just thirty-nine years after Columbus's first voyage, the story of Nuestra Señora de Guadalupe begins in Mexico. On that day Juan Diego, an Aztec peasant, met a beautiful lady on the hill of Tepayac. She stopped him and spoke, telling him she was the Mother of God. She told him she wanted a church built in her honor. Mary appeared as an Aztec woman and spoke in the Aztec language. She instructed Juan Diego to go to the bishop and tell him of her wishes.

Juan did as Mary asked and approached the bishop's residence. There he was treated with disdain, as he was only an Indian and the bishop and his guards were all Spanish. After being the victim of much mockery, he finally got in to see the bishop and told him of the beautiful lady and of her request. Juan Diego was dismissed as a fanatic.

For the next two days Mary appeared to Juan Diego with

the same request and instructions. Each time he was kept waiting longer at the bishop's residence and subjected to more abuse. On his third visit the bishop told Juan to return to the hill, and if the Lady appeared again, he should ask for a sign that he, the bishop, would recognize. The bishop did not reveal to Juan Diego what that sign was.

The next day was December 12, but before Juan could go to the hill at Tepayac, his uncle became seriously ill and needed a priest. Juan Diego avoided the hill where Mary usually met him and went the other way into town to get the priest. As he was rushing around the hill, Mary appeared. Juan Diego told her he couldn't talk to her because his uncle was dying and needed a priest.

Mary smiled at Juan and said: "Listen and be sure, my dear son, that I will protect you. Do not be frightened or grieved. Do not fear any illness, vexation, anxiety, or pain. Am I not your merciful Mother? Are you not under my protection? Am I not of your kind? Do not be concerned about your uncle's illness; he is not going to die. At this very moment he is cured. Is there anything else that you need?"

Mary then told Juan Diego to pick some flowers from a rosebush that miraculously had appeared on the hill and to take them to the bishop. Juan Diego picked the roses, and Mary arranged them in his tilma, a cloth made from cactus fiber that is worn like a poncho. Juan Diego returned to the bishop's house with his tilma filled with roses. While he was being kept waiting, the guards tried to take the roses. Every time they went to pick one, it seemed to disappear into the tilma.

Finally the bishop sent for him. Juan Diego approached the bishop and opened his tilma to let the roses fall on the floor. As he did so, the bishop fell to his knees in astonishment, not at the roses but at the tilma. On it was the picture of the Lady. Juan Diego looked down at his own tilma and exclaimed, "That's the Lady!"

The roses were a special kind that only grew in Castile, Spain. They were the sign that the bishop had asked for. Juan

Diego repeated to the bishop what the Lady had said about the church to be built at Tepayac. He told the story of what the Lady had said about his uncle. Together they returned to his home to find the uncle perfectly well, healed at the very moment Mary had promised.

The church Mary had asked for was built. Devotion to Our Lady of Guadalupe spread. Soon after this, millions of Aztecs who had formerly rejected Christianity became Christians.

Almost five hundred years later Juan Diego's tilma with the image of Mary is still intact. Scientists have examined it and found the fibers as perfect as they would have been the day the tilma was made. Usually cactus fibers disintegrate within a year. For all those years people have gone to see the tilma, to pray at the site of Mary's apparition to Juan Diego, to kneel at the feet of their merciful Mother.

The conquistadors tried to force Christianity upon the Aztecs and failed. Mary came among them as one of them, a powerless Aztec woman. She came without threat or force, carrying only mercy and compassion. Mary came with the power of her love and gathered people under that love for her Son. On December 12 we celebrate Mary, the Christ-bearer to the Americas.

Jesus, heart of mercy, offer us as living sacrifices to God.

Reflection

1. "Am I not your merciful mother?" Is Mary saying this to me? Is Mary saying this to my brothers and sisters?

2. Mary appeared to a poor man. Do I expect the presence of God among the poor and outcast? Do I recognize Christ disguised as a foreigner?

3. Many Aztecs converted to Christianity after the appearance of Mary to Juan Diego. Why? Why did the conquistadors fail to convert many?

WAR TOYS AS PRESENTS
FOR CHILDREN

The American Medical Association has listed violence as a health hazard. The Atlanta Center for Disease Control released statistics in 1991 which revealed that one in five high school students in this country carries a weapon.

Both reports are alarming, and we adults are responsible. We are responsible to our children for the violence we have brought into their environment, for the accessibility of weapons. We are responsible to God for what we have done to our children that they turn to guns and force so easily.

Children have to be taught to use violence. They have to be exposed to ways of using weapons before they know how to use them. Children have to be taught to hate, to be intolerant of differences, to be afraid of the unknown.

As we pray our way through another Advent, preparing for the coming of the Prince of Peace, perhaps we adults need to take the responsibility that is ours for the actions of our children. Not only parents but all adults are responsible for all children. We need to accept this responsibility by giving our children alternatives to violence.

We need to introduce our children to Jesus Christ, the Man of Peace. Our children need to see us as people of peace who use patience and care in our interactions with them and with one another. If we want to teach our children not to use guns and weapons, then they will have to see us not using them or even owning them. We must also teach the children that guns and stealth bombers and army jeeps are not toys, even if they are made of plastic. We must teach them that it isn't safe to pretend to use a gun or a knife to hurt someone else. In a few short years these toddlers will be among the high school students for whom guns are no longer just toys.

If we teach children the true message of Christ, then they might realize that war toys don't belong under the same Christmas tree as the manger scene. They might understand that the love of enemies and the killing of enemies are incompatible.

The important element here is that we adults understand. The children will want whatever toy is popular; they don't care how much it costs or what violence it may be encouraging. They will want it because all their friends have it. We have to love our children enough not to give in to the pressure. They will have to learn that tough decisions and unpopular stands are necessary in life, and that values cannot be sacrificed for fads.

War is not a game. Guns and knives are not toys. If children are going to learn these two important facts, they must start leaning them from the beginning. As responsible members of society, we ought to teach our children the difference between weapons and toys. As Christians, we ought to teach our children to celebrate the birth of the Prince of Peace with gifts and presents that speak of peace.

Jesus, teacher of peace, offer us as living sacrifices to God.

Reflection

1. Are there guns in my home? What does their presence say to children? What does it say to me? Did Christ carry a weapon?

2. Is there violence in my home—physical, emotional, or psychological? Why do I tolerate it? Where can I go for help? When will I go?

3. What kind of presents am I giving to the children on my Christmas list? What do these presents say about my values? Do they reflect Christ's values?

ADVENT: INTRODUCTION

Jesus, Prince of Peace, make us people of peace.

We, the people of God, are sent on mission to bring the good news of peace and redemption to all people. To receive the word of God is to commit ourselves to spread that word Christmas, then, is not a time to focus only on Christ's coming into our hearts individually but also on his coming to us communally. Together we prepare for the advent of the Son of God, and together we share the advent of the Son of God.

Isaiah starts the season by calling us to shed our old skins of defensiveness and hatred and to risk conversion. We work hard at this conversion. It isn't a magic act; it doesn't just happen because we have said a prayer or two. We let go of arrogance, criticism, and self-righteousness and try to live in justice, tolerance, and peace. Before the swords can be beat into plowshares, they have to become unnecessary. Only love makes weapons useless. *Jesus, promise of the ages, make us people of peace.*

In Jesus, peace is possible. The message of Micah is that society pays no attention to the poor and marginalized but looks on their powerlessness as weakness. In Jesus, all things are possible: the powerless become the leaders, the weak become the strong. The victims of oppression can bring about not only their own freedom but the freedom of their oppressors. Christianity turns things upside down so they come out right. We ought to be more surprised by it than we are. This week we travel with the poor, the '*anawim* of God, to prepare for the one who was born in a stable. *Jesus, shepherd of the 'anawim, make us people of peace.*

Halfway through Advent we focus on the prophetic mission of John the Baptist and the prophetic mission of each baptized Christian. John was the last great prophet to announce the Messiah. We, like John, are called to speak the word of God in fidelity and truth. John spoke this not just in words but by his life. We speak of God not just in words but by our lives. We speak of God by the choices we make, by the way we spend our time, and by the way we spend our money. *Jesus, forger of prophets, make us people of peace.*

At the moment when Mary conceived Jesus, she surrendered herself to God. This attitude of abandonment was Mary's preparation for the first Christmas. The scent of jasmine rose in Bethlehem from a woman passionately in love with her God, willing to give birth to the Son of her God. Our final days of preparation for Christmas must be the same—surrender, abandonment, passion, desire, and always jasmine. *Jesus Emmanuel, Son of Mary, make us people of peace.*

ISAIAH

As no other prophet can, Isaiah brings us into Advent. He prepares us as he tried to prepare the people of Israel. Isaiah is a mountain man. He is a guide on the mountain of Yahweh:

> In days to come
>   the mountain of the Lord's house
> shall be established as the
>   highest of the mountains,
> and shall be raised above the hills;
> all the nations shall stream to it (Isaiah 2:2).

> On this mountain the Lord of hosts
>   will make for all peoples
> a feast of rich food, a feast
>   of well-aged wines.
> And he will destroy on this mountain
>   the shroud that is cast over all peoples (Isaiah 25:6f.).

The prophet says, "Come, let us go up to the mountain of the Lord" (Isaiah 2:3). Let us follow Isaiah our guide to see what the view is from the top of the mountain and to learn the dangers and beauties that are part of the climb. It's the beginning of the Advent Season; we must begin or we will not reach the top in time for Christmas.

Blind people can climb mountains as well as the deaf and the paralyzed; young and old people can climb. The separation between rich and poor is insignificant on this climb because we all have to travel light, without excess baggage. The only thing we have to carry is the desire for God. We have to long to meet God at the top or we won't endure. There are no chair lifts or helicopter rides up this mountain. Each of us is responsible for taking that first step. As we travel we also become responsible for helping others.

Isaiah gives us three challenges we will meet along the way. The first challenge is to learn what is not of God, to avoid the paths that lead nowhere. The second is to be willing to change direction in order to find the right path. We have to be willing to be converted, to be turned around, to have the scales fall from our eyes and our paralysis taken away. The last challenge is to learn the ways of God; this is God's mountain and only God knows the way to ascend it. If our goal is God, our means must also be from God.

The Ways That Are Not of God

It is a help to know what doesn't work; it frees us from wasting time pursuing those ways. It is a help to know false claims, because they can be dismissed as irrelevant. False promises can be disregarded before they become a source of disappointment.

Written thousands of years ago, Isaiah's criticism of false religion sounds similar to the laments of our own time. As the world community mourns the slaughter of people in war and the deaths of millions through starvation, we resonate to the cry of Isaiah: "They shall beat their swords into plowshares, and their spears into pruning hooks; nation shall not lift up the sword against nation, neither shall they learn war any more" (Isaiah 2:4). War is not of God.

False religion is that which allows the oppression of those who are weaker. This is an offense to the holiness of Yahweh. Yahweh is coming to wipe away every tear and to destroy the arrogant. Judgment, criticism, living high up in the steep citadel are not the ways of Yahweh. Arrogant living is not of God.

There is no place for tyrants, for gossip that tries to incriminate others, for bribing judges and taking advantage of the innocent. Those who steal from the poor and oppress them cannot climb. The just always come out on the side of the poor. Lack of concern for the poor is not of God.

Appearances and hearsay are not the basis for our decisions. The appealing idols of silver and gold must be thrown away as the polluted things they are. Consumerism and greed are not of God.

Truth cannot be sacrificed for any reason. We cannot call evil good, and good evil. Is not this the hardest challenge of all? When we want something, we make it a good, justifying evil for our own purposes. Deceit is not of God.

Knowledge is power. To know what is not of God is not a burden; it is an opportunity for freedom and growth. Isaiah's warnings are not threats from God but signposts to help us avoid pitfalls along the way.

The Power to Change

Psychologists say that often people would rather endure pain than make the changes necessary to eliminate it. Our first Advent decision focuses on our willingness to change. Do we want to experience the new life of Christ? Do we want it enough to make changes in our own lives?

Our first reaction to Isaiah's description of false religion could be fear: fear of repentance, fear of letting go. We don't know how to survive without war. We don't know what will happen to our lifestyle if we stop oppressing the poor. We don't know if we can let go of our idols of gold and silver and comfort because we have gotten used to them; we might even be dependent upon them. If we try living in truth, we may have to make decisions that will cost us our friends or our jobs.

Repentance isn't easy; it's a risk. What if God isn't enough to satisfy us? There is no way around this predicament but the way of complete trust in God. We have to believe that God is God and that the ways of God are trustworthy and true and humanly fulfilling.

We learn to walk by walking, to talk by talking. We learn to trust by trusting. Advent is beginning time, time to begin to take the first steps in faith, reaching for the hand of God, which is always waiting for us. Trusting doesn't mean understanding; it means loving God enough to trust, and knowing that God loves us enough to accept our trust. This is where we learn prayer. In prayer we receive light to see what must go and what must be developed. In prayer we enter into the infinity of God and find that not only is God awesome but so also are we. In prayer we find love and discover ourselves as lovable.

In Eucharistic prayer we become present to Christ as he gives himself over for the redemption of all people. If we take only one resolution this Advent, let it be that we will participate in the Eucharist as often as possible. It will give us the courage to accept change and to welcome conversion.

There is power in prayer and there is power in conversion, and their relationship is one of interdependence. More simply, we need to be with Christ to know Christ, and Christ needs to be with us just because he loves us.

The Ways of God, the Promises of God

The reward for allowing ourselves to be changed is life in God. It is wonderful and worth all the effort it requires. Our God is good, and to follow in the way of God is to share in the goodness of God.

Fidelity to our relationship with God propels us on the way of justice. We learn to cry justice and to live justice. In other words, we learn the ways of God. The justice of God is not merely human justice; it is justice tempered with mercy.

We receive more than we deserve, and we learn to give more than we receive.

> The spirit of the Lord God is upon me,
>   because the Lord has anointed me;
> he has sent me to bring good news to the oppressed,
>   to bind up the brokenhearted,
> to proclaim liberty to the captives,
>   and release to the prisoners . . .
> to comfort all who mourn . . .
>   to give them a garland instead of ashes,
> the oil of gladness instead of mourning,
>   the mantle of praise instead of a faint spirit
>   (Isaiah 61:13).

The way of God is the way of peace and the promise of peace. All nations will be part of the plan for peace. Yahweh will remove "the shroud that is cast over all peoples" (Isaiah 25:7). The way up the mountain of God is the way of peace. Peace doesn't just happen without our cooperation. It isn't something that God showers indiscriminately from heaven. God gives the grace for peace, but we have to choose to accept that grace and to act accordingly. We have to be willing to put aside personal hurts and offenses and not give in to bitterness and revenge in order to live peacefully with one another.

Isaiah is strong on what it takes to be a peacemaker—it takes willingness to endure evil with love. There is no getting around the surrender to love that the work of peace requires of us. Every day of our lives is a challenge to live in peace and to reject the violence to which our culture inclines us in all aspects of our lives: raising children, sports, entertainment, politics, business. If we live the way of peace, we will live the promise of peace.

God promises us that the deaf will hear, the blind will see, desert land will become fertile, and the poor will rejoice in their God. Yahweh will dress our wounds and heal our bruises. We will learn to dress one another's wounds and heal one another's bruises. Then we will experience the coming of God in our midst. The yoke will be lifted from our shoulders when we lift it from one another's shoulders. The rod of the oppressor will be broken when we break it. And the gear of battle will be consumed by fire when we throw it into the fire.

The promises of God accompany us all along the path of God. As we begin Advent, we need to sit quietly and teach our children to sit quietly, to think in the presence of God about the journey up the mountain. We have to decide specifically what gear we will leave at the base and what we need to bring with us. We need to consider how we will prepare ourselves to accept conversion.

As we begin to climb we trust God, in whose company we are traveling, to show us the ways of God. We are confident and eager, for "a child has been born for us, a son given to us" (Isaiah 9:6). We will see him at the top of the mountain.

Jesus, promise of the ages, make us people of peace.

Reflection

1. According to Isaiah, war, arrogance, lack of concern for the poor, greed, consumerism, and deceit are not the ways of God. What in my life is not of God?

2. Do I need conversion in my life? in what aspects? Can I pray to accept conversion? How will I pray?

3. How am I a peacemaker? How do I confront and free others? How do I show mercy?

Second Week of Advent

MICAH

The prophet Micah keeps our Advent focus simple. Micah was a peasant and lived a simple life. God chose him to be a spokesman for the one who came among us as a simple carpenter from a small town with no prestigious claim to fame according to worldly standards.

Micah dared to love and to allow himself to be loved by Yahweh. He dared to believe that the powerless will share the power of Yahweh Sabaoth. He heard the word of God calling to the poor and the downtrodden.

In Old Testament times the poor who remained faithful to Yahweh were called the *'anawim*. Micah was the great prophet of the *'anawim*. His message was for the marginalized, those people who didn't quite fit in society. To be part of the *'anawim*, however, meant more than just being at the bottom of the economic heap. The name *'anawim* was given to all who never gave up on God because they knew that God had never given up on them.

The *'anawim* to whom Micah was speaking were those who believed in the promises of God, come what may. The wonder of Micah's prophecy is that he spoke of the Messiah himself as being one of the *'anawim*. The long-awaited King of Israel and Savior of all the world would be of lowly birth and humble existence.

But you, O Bethlehem of Ephrathah,
    who are one of the little clans of Judah,
from you shall come forth for me
    one who is to rule in Israel (Micah 5:2).

Like the people of Israel, we are startled. Pomp and circumstance often surround our practice of religion. Places of
honor are given to the heads of any religious denomination.
Our robes for worship are leftovers from medieval aristocracy.
We judge one another by the way we dress and where we live
and the schools we attend, and we are more interested in these
values than in the way we live with God and with one another. We slip into being elitist, even in our faith.

Micah comes again this Advent to help us see more clearly;
he comes to help us avoid the temptation to look good rather
than to be good. We listen as he reassures us that need is not
an impediment to God.

The lame I will make the remnant,
    and those who were cast off, a strong nation (Micah 4:7).

It is hard to believe that powerlessness is the only power
in the kingdom of God. We know how to survive; powerlessness is not the way. Powerlessness can never bring about the
reign of God. It is reasonable not to use force on good people,
but we have to use it on evil ones or we endanger ourselves
and our children. Not according to Micah. He reminds us
of God's promise to save us through powerlessness. The Incarnation is all about the impossible becoming possible. God
became human, and because of that, humanity can become
Godlike. God chose to redeem the world through one who
dared to live a simple life.

Jesus never ran for political office. He never held a position of prestige or honor in his church, the synagogue. He
never even had a permanent address once he began his public life. His disciples were the blue-collar workers of Galilee.
He spent his time with outcasts—lepers, prostitutes, tax col-

lectors, mentally disturbed people, Roman soldiers, and foreigners.

Jesus was a scandal in his time by trying to redeem the world by love alone, without force or violence, without political, economic, or social power. Jesus lived what Micah prophesied. He came as a shepherd to care for his flock. He came to lift up the lowly by being one of them. He came to put down the mighty from their high places by refusing to be one of them.

Micah came with curses for the arrogant and proud of heart and with promises for the lowly and gentle of spirit. God does not need extravagant sacrifices of silver and gold, gifts beyond the reach of poor folks. Micah tells us what is needed to please Yahweh; it is simple and all-consuming at the same time.

> What does the Lord require of you
>   but to do justice, and to love kindness,
>   and to walk humbly with your God? (Micah 6:8).

Do Justice

Micah's cries of justice reverberate with immediacy like newspaper headline stories. He rails against judges who take bribes, priests who are unfaithful and untruthful, the rich who continue to make money at the expense of the poor, and those who steal from the poor by cheating them in business.

It's not enough for us to look at these warnings and start putting names and places on the specific complaints. We must go further and see how we have contributed to the injustice around us. For every person who committed a sinful act, there are many others who knew about it and said nothing. We are responsible both for our actions and for our failures to act. To cooperate with evil by not standing courageously for the truth is to become part of the evil.

Let us pray, first of all, to see injustice for what it is, and then to make an effort to remove it. This is the way of the

Messiah who was promised us. The Just One came into our midst to justify us, to make all of us just, and to teach us to become people of the peaceable kingdom, the kingdom of justice.

Love Kindness

We cannot even strive for justice unless we experience love for those who are being unjustly treated. A passion for justice comes from loving others as our brothers and sisters. Micah shows us a God of great kindness and tenderness.

Yahweh promises us salvation through One who will gather his scattered people. The Messiah "shall stand and feed his flock" (Micah 5:4); he will restore the people of God oppressed in so many ways, and "he shall be the one of peace" (Micah 5:5).

It is amazing that after all the sins of the people of God in Old Testament times and after all the sins of people in our time, God still comes in kindness, promising forgiveness.

God comes to gather us back into the fold and to feed and care for us. Perhaps if we allow ourselves to feel the tenderness of God, we will be moved to act kindly to one another. Wouldn't it be a wonderful Christmas if to each person to whom we give a gift we also promised the gift of kindness and gentleness throughout this year? Wouldn't it be wonderful if we gave our children gifts of interest and care and time and listening?

Wouldn't we be happier this Christmas if we acknowledged the kindness and concern that others show us as we acknowledge the material gifts they give us? It is rude not to thank someone who gives a gift. Do we thank those who, in the course of any ordinary day, meet us with a smile and an act of kindness?

If there are those who meet us without kindness or with injustice, can we not, as God did, still meet them with mercy and love? I know a man who was fired unjustly. At the moment he was fired he said nothing but reached out to shake the hand of the man who fired him before he left the office. The man who was fired is pursuing all the grievance procedures available to him to regain his job, but he is not expressing bitterness toward his employer. Loving tenderly is not for the weak; it is an attribute of the strong.

Walk Humbly with Your God

Only the strong can be gentle in the face of evil, violence, or rejection. Only those who walk with God can be strong, and only they can walk like God in love and mercy.

In the biblical story of creation, God is shown as walking in the cool of the day in the garden of paradise with Adam and Eve (Genesis 3:8). Sin destroyed this relationship, but through God's own Son we have a chance to be redeemed from our banishment. Paradise may not be here on this earth yet, but God did walk among us again through Jesus; and because of this, God still walks with us if we wish it.

At the dawn of day, in the heat of noon, or in the cool of the evening, our God walks with us. We talk of serious things that concern us or give us anxiety; and we talk of the simple details that aren't earth-shattering but are of interest or importance to us and therefore to our God. We speak of our pain and our joys, of life and death, of loneliness and love. We speak of our friends and families, of those we know and of those who are unknown to us. We speak of our children and our parents, of doubts and hopes. To walk simply or humbly with God means to do all things conscious of God's loving presence.

Not only do we need to speak with God, but God needs to speak with us. As we walk, we hear of God's hopes and plans; we hear of God's friends and of God's longing for those who think themselves enemies of God. We hear of God's desire for the children of God to live as one. We walk in the wake of power and majesty, and we know we belong to this God. The One who "shall judge between many peoples, and shall arbitrate between strong nations" is walking with us.

The One who has promised that "nation shall not lift up sword against nation" and that "neither shall they learn war any more" walks with us (Micah 4:3).

To celebrate Christmas means to act as people who know that Christ is among us, to act as people who know that we walk with God, and to treat others as people who know that they also are called to walk with God.

> Come let us go up to the mountain of the Lord . . .
>   that we may walk in God's paths (Micah 4:2).

Jesus, shepherd of the 'anawim, make us people of peace.

Reflection

1. Micah reflects that the Savior will be a poor man without power. Is power important to me? Is prestige important to me? Am I ever tempted to look good rather than be good? How does this temptation come?

2. What call for justice do I hear? Have I prayed over this call? Have I acted on this call?

3. Is my God gentle and kind? Am I gentle and kind? Do I walk with God daily to learn from God's gentleness and kindness?

JOHN THE BAPTIST

John, the son of Elizabeth and cousin of Jesus, was a strange man. His clothes would have won him a place among the "Ten Worst Dressed" in the world of fashion. His diet wouldn't have attracted company to dinner. Like so many of our own poor, his permanent address was vague: "the desert."

Politically John wasn't too smart, for he aggravated Herod by publicly criticizing his marriage. That cost John his head. Who wants to hear some guy always telling you to repent? He didn't even have the satisfaction of being sure that he had prepared the way for the Messiah. While in prison, John had to send out friends to ask Jesus if he was the One who was to come or if they should wait for someone else.

Yet Jesus said of John, "I tell you, among those born of women no one is greater than John" (Luke 7:28). We can learn something from this strange man, John, who was so respected and loved by Jesus.

John the Prophet

John was sent by God as the last great prophet announcing the coming of the Messiah. It was part of God's plan that John speak out and then step aside. John's role in salvation is similar to ours, so it will help if we understand his place in history.

Prophets are people chosen by God to speak the word of God in fidelity and truth. They do this by their lifestyle. Prophecy is more a job description than an experience of foretelling future events. Prophecy is very practical, part of daily life, and usually is not accompanied by extraordinary signs.

How do we know that we are called to be prophets? That's simple: at our baptism we were given the responsibility of living as prophets. Every Christian is a prophet. This isn't something reserved for the exceptional people of our day. We are all called to the role.

Let's look at John as prophet to see what prophecy entails. If Jesus said John was the best, we can learn from him. First of all, John's whole focus in life was preparing for Jesus. It was as if John measured every decision in his life against the criterion, "Will this next step I am going to take prepare for the Messiah?" John's decisions to live in the desert, to wear clothing made of camel's hair, to eat locusts and wild honey, to preach truth fearlessly were all geared to announcing the presence of God.

Wearing clothes made of camel's hair and eating locusts in the desert did not make John a great prophet, and they will not make us great prophets. John's external actions were important because they kept his focus on what was important. Our external actions are important because they express what is important to us. John's particular actions led to the openness of heart and clarity of vision that prepared the people of his day to recognize and welcome the Lord when he came.

Our Call to Be Prophets

In our day we must listen to the inspirations of God in our hearts to know how to be ready and waiting so that the Lord will not go by us unnoticed. It might be that we have to look at where we live and how we dress and what we eat to see if any of these things are blocking the welcome we want to give to the Christ in our midst.

The hardest part of living our lives as prophets is clearing out the clutter surrounding us so that Christ can be seen. We start with the material clutter and move to the clutter of heart, which is so much more subtle. There is something to be said for going to the desert. Shopping malls and NFL games and VCRs have to be left behind when we journey to the desert.

We need to consider two very fundamental and practical ideas at this point in order to accept responsibility for prophecy in our day. These considerations won't guarantee a straight road to Christ or for Christ, but they will level out a few bumps along the way.

The first consideration is time. Like John, let us take the time to go to the desert these last weeks of Advent. Let us take the time to pray and reflect on the coming of Christ in our midst. The desert can be a bedroom, an attic, a cellar, or a living room. It can be a church or a park. The desert is a place where in silence and in solitude we can consider the infinite love of God for us and where we can let this love form our actions.

The second practical suggestion concerns treasure. Why not give alternative Christmas gifts this year? Many of us say that we don't need anything; we already have more than we need, and so do our children and grandchildren. Yet it is fun and special to give a gift; it's a way of telling people that we care about them. So give gifts that can later be given to others in need. For example, give your husband a size three snowsuit or give your teenage son a pair of new sneakers for a toddler. Bring your children to the toy store to pick out presents for needy children. Instead of filling a shopping cart with trinkets that never get used, stock up on warm socks and underwear for the homeless.

After all have opened their presents and all the thanks and hugs are exchanged, make a trip to deliver the presents to those in need. No one is deprived in this exchange; the pleasure of the gifts is that they are given twice.

While I was giving blood a few days before Christmas, the nurse asked for the name and address of a poor family.

She explained that in her family this year they decided to put a ten-dollar limit on the presents that would be exchanged among themselves. She said that they didn't need any more possessions than they had. The rest of the money that they ordinarily would have spent they were giving to the poor.

Another woman gave her family a list of things she wanted for Christmas. On her list were things such as a doll for a six-year-old girl, a sweater for a teenager, a pair of skates for an eleven-year-old boy. The family purchased and wrapped the gifts and gave them to her. They were then given again to a family that could use them.

Metanoia—A Change of Mind

None of these ideas are earth-shattering. None will be enough to bring about the conversion John calls for, but they are a start, a step toward the truth.

The word John uses to express conversion is *metanoia,* which means "a change of mind." This is far more than mere repentance for the sins we know are sins. This is a call for a personal revolution. Yes, we need to repent, but we also need to think differently, to desire differently, and to be motivated differently. Simply stated, we are called to be reborn.

John preached this message of personal conversion very clearly and passionately. He roused people to make that first personal act in their own moral revolution—stepping out from the crowd to be baptized. Making that declaration of intent was crucial to being baptized by John. It was a personal decision, not a group movement. One by one people showed that they were willing to respond to God.

Jesus came into this scene of baptism and, despite John's objections, was baptized himself. Jesus verified the importance of what John was doing and showed the value of following the will of God.

This baptism of John's was not a ritual fulfillment of the letter of some specific law. It was a personal symbol of conversion to God, of entering into a relationship with God. And that is what the sacrament of baptism should be.

In his own ministry Jesus did not baptize. It was unnecessary, since the relationship with God that John's baptism expressed was being lived by Jesus' followers through their relationship with him. Only after the death of Jesus did the disciples begin baptizing in his name.

A Step Toward the Messiah

The passage of years does not diminish either the essential commitment or the essential power of our baptism. Even if we were baptized as infants, it is still our responsibility, and still within our power, to live daily our baptismal call. This means that we live, first of all, in the experience of being chosen and called and loved by an infinitely compassionate and generous God. And it means that we continually step from the crowd to acknowledge our beliefs.

In today's society teenagers are often immobilized by peer pressure. It takes tremendous courage on their part to make personal decisions that may not be popular with or accepted by their group. We are quick to recognize this in our youth. What we are less quick to recognize and admit is our own inability to break free from the subtle standards of society. We expect teenagers to walk away from illegal drugs and illicit sex, but we do not walk away from off color jokes, racist remarks, or dishonest business deals. We want our kids to be respectful when we talk to them, but we are not always respectful to them. Sometimes we are cruel and abusive.

All of us need to practice stepping from the crowd into closer relationship with Christ. We don't experience this relationship with Jesus automatically by joining the Church or by following a set of rules, especially if at the same time we are ignoring our neighbor in need. Relationship with Jesus comes from being with Jesus, learning from Jesus, and practicing the ways of Jesus.

At this point on our Advent journey, let us pray for the graces we need to live out our baptismal commitment. In gratitude we approach God for sharing infinity with us, for sharing divinity with us. In faith we believe that the ways of Jesus are practical and possible. In hope we put aside the standards of the world about us. Finally, in love we dare to touch the incarnate God in our brothers and sisters.

Jesus, forger of prophets, make us people of peace.

Reflection

1. How do I live my baptismal call to be a prophet? What is God speaking to me? How do I in turn speak this truth to others?

2. What values does my lifestyle reflect? my neighborhood? my friends? my clothes? my expenses? Am I able to find a desert this Advent and reflect on these external expressions of internal values?

3. Do I believe that I am loved by an infinitely compassionate and generous God? How do I express this belief? Do I step from the crowd to proclaim this belief? What is my step? Where is my crowd?

Fourth Week of Advent

MARY

Look, the virgin shall conceive and bear a son,
and they shall name him Emmanuel (Matthew 1:23).

Christmas is our celebration of the union of the passion of God with the passion of Mary in the person of Jesus Christ. We can celebrate Christmas this year in joy and happiness and peace regardless of the pain or suffering or emptiness in our own lives.

Today psychologists, sociologists, and ordinary people often speak of the stress of the holidays. Commercialism raises expectations of a togetherness that many people do not experience. But regardless of our situation, we don't have to experience Christmas as a time when we are programmed into false ideas of happiness, only to be left sulking in their unfulfillment.

Christmas is about the birth of Christ; nothing else added to the feast is essential. We know that Christ was born in Bethlehem two thousand years ago, and we believe he will be born in us again if we allow him. With this we have all that is necessary for the celebration of the feast.

So let the celebration begin. In the company of Mary we plan our Christmas. We prepare, we invite others to join us, and we give and receive gifts.

Prepare the Stable for Christ

Mary prepared for the coming of Christ long before she arrived in Bethlehem and began searching for a place to stay for the night. Mary was a being in anticipation, a person wholly given to the presence of God in her life. Her life was open and receptive to the will of God, however God chose to make that will known.

At the moment Mary conceived Jesus, she surrendered herself to God. She said that she would be willing to be used by God in any way God desired to use her. This attitude of abandonment was Mary's preparation for the first Christmas. We need to understand it well if we are to prepare for Christmas as she did.

We see Mary giving uncompromising obedience to the will of God, even when she didn't know what to do about telling Joseph that she was pregnant. Trust God with the details and all will be well. Dreams and angels will enter into our lives if we allow them.

Surely Mary had prepared a place in Nazareth for her new baby. Circumstances brought the young couple to Bethlehem instead. Trust God with the details and all will be well. Prophecy was fulfilled in the city of David and a child was born.

When Herod Archelaus tried to kill the infant Jesus in Bethlehem, Mary and Joseph were afraid to go home to Nazareth, because Galilee was under the rule of his brother, Herod Antipas. So they fled into Egypt instead, and again prophecy was fulfilled. Trust God with the details and all will be well. In God's time they would be back in their own land.

Hard decisions, difficult days on the road, separation from family and friends, openness to the stranger, whether Magi or shepherd—this is the way Mary prepared for the birth of the Christ, giving priority to God in her life. Such must be our way of preparing also. We must decide to give the ways of God priority in our lives. That means hard decisions about the use of our time, resources, and talents, decisions that are difficult and may separate us from our family and friends. Trust God with the details and all will be well.

When Mary and Joseph finally arrived at the site where Christ was to be born, they must have done many things to prepare for the birth of Jesus. Can we not imagine the love and excitement with which they prepared? We can find the same love and excitement in our preparations.

It has been a custom since the time of St. Francis of Assisi to set up a stable scene with manger, shepherds, and animals. We can enjoy setting up the crib in our homes and then ask ourselves if our use of time, treasure, and talents is consistent with it.

If we set up the crib a few days early, we will have a reminder of the need to prepare. If we keep the manger scene before our eyes, it can keep us from being swept away by the last minute rush of commercialism. The manger scene slows us down by focusing us on essentials. As children we used to be taught that the straws for the manger came from our acts of kindness. That's not bad theology if we consider the core of the teaching, which is that the way to prepare for the coming of Christ is to act like Christ toward one another. A wonderful aspect of being Christian is that what we do for one another we do for Christ. This is not symbolism but reality.

Inviting Company to Celebrate

In the spirit of love for one another, we invite others to join us as we celebrate this feast of love. In some families it is a custom to put candles in the window on Christmas so that Christ can find the way to their house. According to legend, Christ comes in the guise of a stranger in need of shelter. We can put a candle in at least one window to remind ourselves to let in the stranger. It's possible that the stranger could be someone in our own family or someone we have known for many years. Praying to the Holy Spirit for inspiration, we ask for eyes to recognize Christ hidden in others and for hearts to welcome them into our homes.

Part of the process of praying for this is to take time to think about whom we might invite to celebrate some part of

Christmas with us. There might be an elderly person who needs a ride to church on Christmas. Perhaps someone in our neighborhood would like to join us as we go to Mass. If we go visiting for Christmas, is there someone in a hospital or nursing home whom we can stop off to see? A neighbor with children might appreciate adult company for coffee and rolls. A phone call can make a lonely person feel good.

If we are too busy on Christmas for these simple acts of human love, we are busy at things that are not Christmas. To go through the holiday without plans to express love and live the message of Christmas is to fail to prepare for the day. Let us stay close to Mary, not in her plaster statue image but in her reality as a young woman who endured hardship and risked her reputation to become the Mother of God.

Gift-Giving

We stay close to Mary especially during the final hours before the feast. Last-minute shopping in crowded supermarkets and shopping malls can smother any sense of the holiness and awesomeness of the event we are commemorating. The antidote to such suffocation of spirituality is simple: stay away from the commercialism of the marketplace by staying away from the marketplace.

A comfortable chair in front of the lighted Christmas tree is a good place to say a quiet rosary or to listen to religious carols. We can savor moments of graced solitude; we can even find them in the midst of a busy family. If emptiness seems to fill our life, we can fill the emptiness with prayer. Instead of fearing the loneliness, we can let the beads slip through our fingers and be at home with Mary on this most holy day.

The spirit and mood of Christmas were not invented by Currier and Ives or Norman Rockwell. Christmas is the birth of the incarnate Word of God in human history. No pain or misery or tragedy is great enough to limit the effectiveness of this day. Christmas is not something we feel; it is Someone we choose to believe in and to hope in, no matter what the circumstances of our lives might be this Christmas.

The gift of Christmas is Christ—to be given and received. Mary first gave us Christ through her own body. There can be no disappointment or letdown following her gift because there is, in a sense, no end to this day. Every day is the day of Christ's presence among us. Every day of Mary's life, from the moment of Jesus' conception in her, was given to her Son and to receiving and sharing his message.

Like Mary, we carry within us the seed of new life. We bring Christ to those we meet each day, and we receive Christ from other Christ-bearers. Every day gives us opportunities to express this mysterious, wondrous reality. On Christmas we celebrate this mystery and this alone. All other things that have become part of the Christmas tradition belong there only in the measure that they help us to appreciate life in Christ. If they do not contribute to this appreciation, they are not necessary.

If we celebrate Christmas for what it is and not for the trappings that have accumulated through the years, we cannot be depressed or dejected. We are welcoming the Son of God into our midst. We are preparing and celebrating in the presence of his Mother. We rejoice and sing and dance because it is a great and wonderful thing that God is with us and we with God. Let us sweep our paths, open our doors, and receive in our arms the God of all ages and all people. The Holy One, the Prince of Peace, the Light of Lights is among us. "Glory to God in the highest heaven, and on earth peace among those whom he favors" (Luke 2:14).

Jesus Emmanuel, Son of Mary, make us people of peace.

Reflection

1. How am I preparing for Christmas? What are the difficult details of my daily life that I must use to prepare a stable for Christ? Am I giving priority to God and not to my wor-

ries and anxieties? What was Mary's abandonment? What is mine?

2. Is there a manger scene in my home? Is it there because of custom, or is it an expression of the meaning of Christmas for me? Do I pray in front of it? How can I use the manger to remind me of Christ's presence?

3. Will time in the shopping malls suffocate the simplicity of Christ's presence? How can I avoid commercialism? What Christmas traditions make me conscious of being a Christ-bearer? Do I allow the wonderful mystery of God's becoming human to dwell in my heart?

NOTES

1. Martin Luther King, Jr., *Strength to Love* (Philadelphia, Fortress Press, 1963) 54.
2. Martin Luther King, Jr., *Why We Can't Wait* (New York: New American Library, 1964) 79.
3. Paul Glynn, *A Song For Nagasaki* (Hunter's Hill, Australia: The Catholic Book Club, 1990) 26.
4. *The Liturgy of the Hours* (New York: Catholic Book Publishing Co., 1975) 1664.
5. Etty Hillesum, *An Interrupted Life: The Diaries of Etty Hillesum, 1941-1943* (New York: Washington Square Press, 1985) 207, 237, 159, 188.
6. T. S. Eliot, *Murder in the Cathedral* (New York: Harcourt, Brace & World, 1963) 11.
7. Ibid., 73.
8. Some of this material is taken, with permission of the publishers, from Patricia McCarthy, C.N.D., "Called to Praise," *Marian Helpers Bulletin,* vol. 47, no. 4).
9. For information on the Catholic bishops' opposition to the death penalty, see JUSPAX, U.S. Catholic Conference, 1312 Massachusetts Ave. N.W., Washington, D.C., 20005, phone (202) 659-6797.
10. For information on death penalty statistics, see Amnesty International U.S.A., Publications Dept., 322 Eighth Ave., New York, N.Y., 10001.
11. Some of this material is taken, with permission of the publishers, from Patricia McCarthy, C.N.D., "Mary, Woman for Peacemakers" (*Review for Religious,* vol. 50, no. 3, May–June, 1991).
12. Terry Anderson, in a personal letter to the author, April 2, 1992.

13. Bishops' Committee on the Liturgy, *Environment and Art in Catholic Worship* (Washington, D.C.: United States Catholic Conference, 1978) no. 101.

14. Andrew Greeley, *Faithful Attraction* (New York: A Tom Doherty Associates Book, 1992) 77, 229, 234.

15. e. e. cummings, *W (Vi Va) 1931 LVII, Complete Poems* (New York: Harcourt, Brace & Jovanovich, Inc., 1972) 336.

16. This fast was begun in 1983 by Fr. Emmanuel Charles McCarthy. For information concerning this fast, contact Olive Branch Communications, 106 Almy Street, Providence, RI 02909.

17. All the quotes in this section are taken from filmed interviews with the atomic bomb scientists recorded in the film *The Day After Trinity* (California, KTEH San Jose Productions).

18. Sister Kayoko Shibata, excerpts from a sermon at Trinity Test Site in Socorro, New Mexico, July 16, 1992.

19. Paul Glynn, *A Song For Nagasaki* (Hunter's Hill, Australia: The Catholic Book Club, 1990) 126.

20. For further insights into Mary's assumption, see David M. Knight, *Mary in an Adult Church* (Memphis, Tenn.: His Way, Inc., 1988).

21. Mahatma Gandhi, *Gandhi on Non-Violence,* ed. Thomas Merton (New York: New Directions, 1964) 40.

22. Aline D. Wolfe, *The Challenge of Maria Montessori* (Altoona, Penn.: Parent Child Press, 1989) 37.

23. David M. Knight, *Sacred Heart Church Bulletin* (Memphis, Tenn., January 31, 1993).

24. A. J. Muste, *Gandhi and the H-Bomb* (New York, Fellowship Publications, 1992) 9.

25. Mahatma Gandhi, *Gandhi on Non-Violence,* ed. Thomas Merton (New York: New Directions, 1965) 26.

26. Ibid., 6.

27. Ibid., 45.

28. Mahatma Gandhi, *All Men Are Brothers* (New York: Continuum Publishing Corp., 1982) 88.

29. The Stations of the Cross are another example of a devotion used for political purposes. They originally started as a way of supporting the Crusades. Despite their dubious origin, they can be a powerful experience of sharing in the passion of Christ.

30. Robert Ellsberg, ed., *Dorothy Day, Selected Writings* (Maryknoll, N.Y.: Orbis Books, 1992) 92.